THE VOICE OF THE
BRIDE

THE VOICE OF THE BRIDE

ENTERING OUR IDENTITY, ANOINTING, AND KINGDOM PURPOSE FOR THE LAST DAYS

PAUL KEITH DAVIS

DESTINY IMAGE® PUBLISHERS, INC.

P.O. Box 310, Shippensburg, PA 17257-0310

"Promoting Inspired Lives."

This book and all other Destiny Image and Destiny Image Fiction books are available at Christian bookstores and distributors worldwide.

Cover design by Eileen Rockwell
Interior design by Terry Clifton

For more information on foreign distributors, call 717-532-3040.
Reach us on the Internet: www.destinyimage.com.

ISBN 13 TP: 978-0-7684-6015-5
ISBN 13 eBook: 978-0-7684-6016-2
ISBN 13 HC: 978-0-7684-6018-6
ISBN 13 LP: 978-0-7684-6017-9

For Worldwide Distribution, Printed in the U.S.A.
1 2 3 4 5 6 7 8 / 26 25 24 23 22

CONTENTS

CHAPTER 1

A MESSENGER FROM THE UNSEEN REALM

THERE ARE MANY voices in this present generation. There is the voice of human reasoning, the voice of innocent blood, the voice of politicians, and even the voice of the martyrs. However, the one voice that has not yet been fully heard is the voice of the Lord's Bride. Revelation 18:23 states:

> *The light of a lamp will not shine in you any longer; and the voice of the bridegroom and bride will not be heard in you any longer; for your merchants were the great men of the earth, because all the nations were deceived by your sorcery.*

This passage clearly outlines a season of time in which the voice of the Bridegroom will be distinctly articulated through His Bride and a specific time for it to cease. Throughout the earth there is a religious and political spirit that the Bible identifies as "Mystery Babylon." Nevertheless, in the midst of this ungodly system the Holy Spirit will release great praise and worship, expressions of God's creative ability, and the distinction of His true voice.

A Mighty Outpouring

A few years ago, while in a conference in Regina, Saskatchewan, I was in prayer for the Sunday morning service. I had been awake for a couple of hours and had propped the pillows against the headboard with my Bible in my lap. I am not certain if I went into a spiritual vision or a trance like Peter experienced in Acts 10, but I suddenly saw an opening appear at the foot of my bed like a large window or door into the unseen realm. Then a man stepped through standing before me at the end of my bed. He was about six feet in height, maybe more, wearing a white robe with light blondish hair. He was very powerful yet not frightening. He reached his right hand toward me and pointed his index finger at me and announced with great authority, "There is about to be a mighty outpouring of the Spirit and it will be the voice of the Bride." With that prophetic proclamation, he vanished.

Although the Church has experienced many expressions of spiritual outpourings, the Bride, the wife of the Lamb, has not yet had her revival. There is a "weighty" presence or glory that the Lord intends to place upon His people during these last days as a testimony to the nations of His authenticity. We are not completely certain what this will look like, but we know that it will transcend the present understanding of God's Word and the working of His Spirit.

> ALTHOUGH THE CHURCH HAS EXPERIENCED MANY EXPRESSIONS OF SPIRITUAL OUTPOURINGS, THE BRIDE, THE WIFE OF THE LAMB, HAS NOT YET HAD HER REVIVAL.

This company will be the literal fulfillment of John 14:12, doing the works the Lord did and even more of them. Like the Lord Jesus, His Bride will be entrusted with the sevenfold Spirit of God operating in fullness to demonstrate God's radiant nature and His great redemptive power.

TWO KINGDOMS

There are two kingdoms operating simultaneously in the earth; the Kingdom of God and the kingdom of satan. The apostle Paul, while sharing his Damascus road experience, reiterated his divine commission. In a face-to-face encounter, the Lord commanded him to open the eyes of the people in order to bring them out of darkness into light and from the dominion of satan into the dominion of God. That is likewise the Bride's commission. He recorded:

To open their eyes so that they may turn from darkness to light and from the dominion of Satan to God, that they may receive forgiveness of sins and an inheritance among those who have been sanctified by faith in Me (Acts 26:18).

Within this world's system, the voice of the Bridegroom will be heard through the Bride in one final demonstration of God's glorious power. While we're in the world we are not of the world. The Holy Spirit in us is the antidote and the remedy for the burdens of this world. The Lord stated in John 17:14-16:

I have given them Your word; and the world has hated them, because they are not of the world, even as I am not of the world. I do not ask You to take them out of the world, but to keep them from the evil one.

Even though the Bride of Christ is required to live within satan's corrupt system for a season, we will enjoy fellowship with God, sovereign protection, and the commission to manifest light in the midst of this darkness. John said it this way:

We know that no one who is born of God sins; but He who was born of God keeps him, and the evil one does not touch him. We know that we are of God, and that the whole world lies in the power of the evil one (1 John 5:18-19).

Jesus emphatically stated that His Kingdom is not of this world, but from another realm (see John 18:36). The Kingdom of Heaven is within the Bride of Christ to manifest righteousness, peace, and joy in one final display of God's glory and power for the great harvest. It will be the voice of the Bride.

THIS IS THE TIME

All prophetic indications point to this spiritual season as the time when the voice of the Bride will be sounded with great clarity and discernment. Over the last one hundred years, the Church has experienced many expressions of revival and spiritual outpouring, but no generation has yet witnessed the spotless Bride who has such intimate fellowship with the Bridegroom that her words are a perfect expression of His heart. The Bridegroom will speak in Heaven and the Bride will echo His voice in the earth.

Modern church history records a progressive restoration of our apostolic heritage and the unfolding of a divine plan that prepares the Bride of Christ without spot or wrinkle. During those seasons, various forerunners provided a prophetic model for the coming corporate body that will function in the full appropriation of God's redemptive qualities. They will not only have the intimate relationship of a bride but will also function in the earth as sons of the Kingdom.

These prophetic forerunners have primarily provided a "John the Baptist" type of ministry to prepare a remnant for divine visitation and restoration to God's people of lost heritages. John, speaking about his role, stated:

> *You yourselves are my witnesses that I said, "I am not the Christ," but, "I have been sent ahead of Him." He who has the bride is the bridegroom; but the friend of the bridegroom, who stands and hears him, rejoices greatly because of the bridegroom's voice. So this joy of mine has been made full* (John 3:28-29).

The prophet Jeremiah also prophesied this saying,

> *"The voice of joy and the voice of gladness, the voice of the bridegroom and the voice of the bride, the voice of those who say, 'Give thanks to the Lord of hosts, for the Lord is good, for His lovingkindness is everlasting'; and of those who bring a thank offering into the house of the Lord. For I will restore the fortunes of the land as they were at first," says the Lord* (Jeremiah 33:11).

FRIENDS OF THE BRIDEGROOM

Many friends of the Bridegroom surfaced during the 20th century exemplifying lives of purity and power that will characterize the last-day Bride of Christ. They called attention to our current place in history and the mandate to come up higher to a place of revelatory insight and spiritual maturity. One of the keys to unlocking this mystery is by honoring the work of God's Spirit through these champions and imitating their faith (see Heb. 13:7-8).

Many of God's people are recognizing and honoring the pioneering work of men and women like A.A. Allen, Alexander Dowie, John G. Lake, Kathryn Kuhlman, William Branham, Maria Woodworth-Etter, and others. In many ways they were spiritual prototypes of the relationship and power to be exemplified by the Bride.

Some of these have been the most dishonored individuals of the 20th-century Church, yet were used most notably in soul winning and the miraculous. Our adversary has effectively attempted to neutralize the testimony of these individuals as forerunners by overly emphasizing their failures and weaknesses. Even so, the Lord is allowing a body of people to recognize the pioneering influence these individuals conveyed in order to position us to carry forward the unfinished commissions.

> THE LORD IS ALLOWING A BODY OF PEOPLE TO RECOGNIZE THE PIONEERING INFLUENCE THESE INDIVIDUALS CONVEYED IN ORDER TO POSITION US TO CARRY FORWARD THE UNFINISHED COMMISSIONS.

I WILL HAVE MY HARVEST

Around the same time I experienced the heavenly messenger, I heard the Lord say, "I *will* have My harvest!" There was great emphasis on the word *"will."* The writings of Daniel and Revelation highlight a mysterious and wonderful book containing mysteries of God's Kingdom and His divine plan for the end-of-time harvest. Revelation 5:9-10 records:

> *And they sang a new song, saying, "Worthy are You to take the book and to break its seals; for You were slain, and purchased for God with Your blood men from every tribe and tongue and people and nation. You have made them to be a kingdom and priests to our God; and they will reign upon the earth."*

This is the book sealed in the days of Daniel to be revealed during the last-day generation containing great insight and understanding vital to our mandate. The angel Gabriel provided these revelations to Daniel in a profound lip-to-ear encounter. We next see this book in the hand of the Father waiting for the One who is worthy to take it from His hand and break its seals.

Only the Lamb that was slain was found worthy to take the book and break its seals to unfold God's complete plan to redeem to Himself men and women from every nation and culture. He will then empower them to function in a priestly role of ministry unto the Lord and delegate His authority as spiritual kings. John was representing the Bride in Revelation 10:10-11, saying:

> *I took the little book out of the angel's hand and ate it, and in my mouth it was sweet as*

honey; and when I had eaten it, my stomach was made bitter. And they said to me, "You must prophesy again concerning many peoples and nations and tongues and kings."

The voice of the Bride will be heard prophesying these great revelations providing the unveiling, disclosure, and the manifestation of the Lord Jesus Christ to every people group on earth. She is not commissioned to merely read them intellectually, but to devour them. She is to become the revelation of Jesus Christ and function like a weapon in God's hand to shatter the strongholds of the enemy and release the spirit of harvest.

> THE VOICE OF THE BRIDE WILL BE HEARD PROPHESYING THESE GREAT REVELATIONS PROVIDING THE UNVEILING, DISCLOSURE, AND THE MANIFESTATION OF THE LORD JESUS CHRIST TO EVERY PEOPLE GROUP ON EARTH.

God is presently operating like a blacksmith, using the pressures of this world and personal circumstances to forge for Himself a weapon for its work that is to bring to ruin the destroyer. Once complete, no weapon will be successful in its attempt to overcome this community of champions (see Isa. 54:16-17).

We will function as both priests and kings through the appropriation of His blood and prophesy to the nations to awaken His purchase of souls. They will be a mature community of radical "overcomers." That is the promise of God's Word.

For the Bride of Christ to be identified with the Bridegroom, she has been required to know something of the wilderness. Song of Solomon portrays the bride coming forth from the desert leaning upon her Beloved. This picture captures our present condition. The Holy Spirit allured us into the wilderness for a time so that He could speak tenderly to us and to the issues of our hearts. Now, from this place we emerge with God's anointing and the power of His Spirit to become the Voice of the Bridegroom trumpeted on earth.

CHAPTER 2

THE BRIDE'S END-TIME HARVEST ANOINTING

ONE OF THE great Old Testament prophecies regarding the promised Messiah is Isaiah 11:1-3. This passage prophetically foretells the anointing resident upon our Redeemer who would usher in a new era in human history. It declares:

> *Then a shoot will spring from the stem of Jesse, and a branch from his roots will bear fruit. The Spirit of the Lord will rest on Him, the spirit of wisdom and understanding, the spirit of counsel and strength, the spirit of knowledge and the fear of the Lord. And He will delight in the fear of the Lord, and He will not judge by what His eyes see, nor make a decision by what His ears hear.*

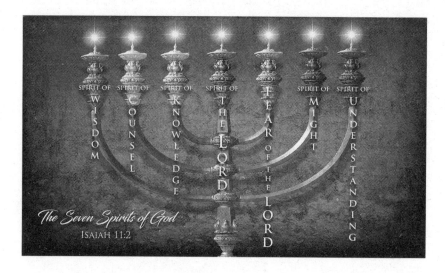

The Seven Spirits of God
ISAIAH 11:2

God's "sevenfold Spirit" is a wonderful mystery to highlight the functioning of the Lord's Spirit in the earth. It is not in contradiction to the triune nature of God but a perfect and complete expression of His Spirit that demonstrates the fullness of His character and power. The Spirit of the Lord doesn't *have* wisdom and revelation, counsel and might, knowledge and reverential awe; He *is* all of these.

The Book of Revelation uses the phrase "Seven Spirits of God" in four passages. It is taken from two Greek words:

- *Hepta*, meaning seven, or more appropriately sevenfold.

- *Pneumata,* meaning a plural rendering of spirits, breath, or wind that can also be used to describe a singular object or person.

The seven aspects of the Holy Spirit provide a clearer definition of His nature. The Spirit of the Lord is an expression of who He is while wisdom and revelation, counsel and might, and knowledge and the reverential fear of God are *what* He is.

The Jewish Bible records Revelation 4:5 as follows:

> *From the throne came forth lightnings, voices and thunderings; and before the throne were seven flaming torches, which are the sevenfold Spirit of God* (CJB).

THE LORD'S MINISTRY

A simple examination of the four Gospels clearly illustrates the functioning of this manifestation of God's Spirit through the One who is our perfect example. However, it does not end there! Astonishingly, the Lord Jesus prophesied that as the Father sent Him, so also does He send us. He goes further, emphasizing the works that He did we shall do also, and even greater works shall we do because He has ascended to the Father. We simply cannot fulfill this responsibility with any anointing less than the full manifestation of the sevenfold Spirit of God.

WE SIMPLY CANNOT FULFILL THIS RESPONSIBILITY WITH ANY ANOINTING LESS THAN THE FULL MANIFESTATION OF THE SEVENFOLD SPIRIT OF GOD.

The Bride of Christ is to be "bone of His bone and flesh of His flesh." The body is to be an extension of the Head. We are called to carry on in these last days the fullness of the Lord's ministry to bring in the harvest of the ages through a many-membered body. The Lord is depicted as a Lamb slain having seven horns and seven eyes, which are the seven Spirits of God. Revelation 5:6 declares:

> *And I looked, and behold, in the midst of the throne and of the four living creatures, and in the midst of the elders, stood a Lamb as though it had been slain, having seven horns and seven eyes, which are the seven Spirits of God sent out into all the earth* (NKJV).

The sevenfold Spirit is a complete representation of His revelation (seven eyes) and power (seven horns) essential to accomplish His plan in the earth. In order for the Church to do the works that He did, fulfilling John 14:12, this same manifestation of the Spirit must also rest upon her! The Lord promised to baptize us in the Holy Spirit and fire; the Seven Spirits of God are manifested in fire.

CONSECRATION AND PREPARATION

It is no small responsibility for someone to be anointed in fullness with the sevenfold Spirit of God. Much prayer and preparatory refining must usher in the release of this powerful spiritual reality. Careful adherence to the leading of the Spirit must also follow in the administration of these mantles of the Spirit's attributes. It will be the responsibility of God's fivefold ministry gifts to prepare the Bride for her end-time anointing. The apostles, prophets, evangelists, pastors, and teachers are given for:

The equipping of the saints for the work of service, to the building up of the body of Christ; until we all attain to the unity of the faith, and of the knowledge of the Son of God, to a mature man, to the measure of the stature which belongs to the fullness of Christ (Ephesians 4:12-14).

There are numerous forerunners who have gone before us as spiritual prototypes to demonstrate a mature life in God and the fullness of His anointing. John G. Lake was described as a 20th-century apostle of faith. Even after experiencing great success in evangelism and the ministry of healings and deliverances, he describes being propelled into a deeper place in God following a nine-month season of prayer and fasting. He did so on a quest to satisfy a profound longing of his soul for more of God. It was there that he discovered the fullness of Christ that catapulted him into a much higher plain of revelation and power clearly demonstrated in the last decades of his life.

His messages vividly outline the progressions that brought him to the place of total surrender to become, as he put it, a "Christ-man." For those who have been so prepared, the Seven Spirits of God will become a reality in this present age. The Church has seen only an isolated few willing to pay the price and endure the persecution to become a mature man with the stature that belongs to the fullness of Christ. Even so, this generation will produce a company of "dread champions" anointed in this way; an invitation is being extended to whosoever will.

DIVINE PAIRS

The Seven Spirits of God work together in pairs. The spirit of wisdom and the spirit of understanding work in harmony with one another. The spirits of counsel and might work in unison as do the spirits of knowledge and reverential fear of God, all flowing from the manifestation of the Spirit of the Lord.

The gifts of the Spirit are appropriations of the Spirit operated by His will when the need arises. We do not possess the gifts; rather, the gifts are manifested according to need. All nine gifts of the Spirit can operate within a believer filled with the Holy Spirit. However, the Seven Spirits of God are measurably greater demonstrations of the Spirit taking the mature and purified believer deep into God's mysteries and power.

The Seven Spirits of God are "mantles" placed upon the believer to operate in full measure. It is a wonderful thing to receive a word of wisdom, but it is altogether greater to walk in the spirit of wisdom. The "mantle" that rested upon Elijah and Elisha was an Old Testament representation of this reality. An examination of the messages and miracles demonstrated in these ministries reveals the functioning of God's sevenfold Spirit. The distinction is that the Spirit descended upon these prophets as the need arose while we are promised an abiding presence that is perpetual.

> IT IS A WONDERFUL THING TO RECEIVE A
> WORD OF WISDOM, BUT IT IS ALTOGETHER
> GREATER TO WALK IN THE SPIRIT OF WISDOM.

The Spirit's anointing that came upon these Old Testament prophets rested for a season until God's mandate was complete and then it lifted; in the ministry of the Lord Jesus the Spirit remained, tabernacled in the Son of God. The Bible declares that the heavens opened and the Holy Spirit descended as the appearance of a dove *and remained.* This is our promise as well!

WISDOM AND REVELATION

For the purposes of this chapter, we will emphasize understanding of wisdom and revelation.

For the release of the mantle of wisdom and understanding, we must pray and ask for it and the integrity to steward it well. The apostle Paul taught us that in Ephesians 1:17-19. Equipping and instruction will result, helping us to appropriately understand the biblical offices and administration. We must earnestly desire these mantles and pray for the maturity, character, and grace to be endowed with them. Their benefits are enormous.

1. The eyes of our hearts enlightened

2. Insight to know what is the hope of His calling

3. What are the riches of the glory of His inheritance in the saints

4. What is the surpassing greatness of His power toward us who believe

The spirit of wisdom is the supernatural ability of God that comes upon our spirits to see Jesus as He is and receive a spiritual understanding and knowledge of God's Word that enables us to know what to do, when to do it, and how to do it in every situation. It also reveals God's manifold and unsearchable wisdom and secrets affecting His plans and purposes. It means a deeper intimacy into the things of God.

The Lord Jesus is seated at the right hand of the Father and the Bride is to be seated with Him in heavenly places. Therefore, this places the Bride at the right hand of the Father with Him. In this place, the Lord can communicate in a moment of time insight that would take many hours and even months to unfold otherwise. If we will learn the art of waiting on God, we will discover the mysteries of the Kingdom through these mantles.

> IF WE WILL LEARN THE ART OF WAITING ON GOD, WE WILL DISCOVER THE MYSTERIES OF THE KINGDOM THROUGH THESE MANTLES.

SPIRIT OF UNDERSTANDING

The spirit of revelation/understanding is a comprehension of the things of God providing understanding with the mind giving insight with perception. Wisdom and understanding provide insight into the true nature of things and the ability to discern mode of action with a view to their results. It is the ability to not only know the things of God but also the application of them practically.

Revelation is the comprehension imparted into our spirits from the Holy Spirit and transmitted into our minds. It is the voice of God speaking to our spirits and informing our minds of that which God is going to do, the unfolding of hidden secrets by the Holy Spirit, and the revealing of mysteries and insight into the future.

Daniel 1:17 and 5:11-12 convey that Daniel was anointed with this same spirit and how it functioned in his life. As with Daniel, it will enable us to understand God's plans and purposes in the unveiling of Himself. Gabriel came to Daniel saying, *"O Daniel, I have now come forth to give you insight with understanding"* (Dan. 9:22).

Following that commissioning, Gabriel divulged tremendous visions with far-reaching implications and then explained their meaning. As demonstrated by this great prophet, humility and an excellent spirit are vital attributes in the operation of the spirits of wisdom and revelation.

> HUMILITY AND AN EXCELLENT SPIRIT ARE VITAL ATTRIBUTES IN THE OPERATION OF THE SPIRITS OF WISDOM AND REVELATION.

OUR MANDATE

The spirits of wisdom and revelation will enable us to understand the deep mysteries and purposes of God that are kept hidden. The apostle Paul stated in Romans 16:25:

> *Now to Him who is able to establish you according to my gospel and the preaching of Jesus Christ, according to the revelation of the mystery which has been kept secret for long ages past.*

Paul's ministry clearly revealed mysteries of the Kingdom with this anointing and mantle of the Holy Spirit. When the spirit of wisdom is resting upon you, deep truths are instantaneously imparted while meditating upon God's Word. The spirit of revelation is then present to give understanding of truth and its relevant application.

Wisdom and understanding provide knowledge of the Godhead and allow us to know God more affectionately. This paves the way to intimate appreciation of God Himself—the inner beauty of the Lord displayed in grace and glory. Likewise, we must adorn the inner man with meekness and humility. The inner beauty of God is His grace—the beauty of holiness. The spirit of wisdom and revelation will give us the comprehension of these aspects of God. As Second Corinthians 3:17 declares:

> *Now the Lord is the Spirit, and where the Spirit of the Lord is, there is liberty.*

CHAPTER 3

SONSHIP: THE WORD AND SPIRIT UNITED

IN JOHN 1, the Bible records that in the beginning the Word existed; then the Word (Logos) became flesh and dwelt among mankind. After 30 years of growth and maturity, the time came for the Lord's work of ministry to fulfill His assignment in the earth. At His baptism, the Bible describes the heavens opened and the Holy Spirit descended as the appearance of a dove. The Word and Spirit were united and the Father declared, "This is My beloved Son." We become the manifested sons when the revealed Word and Spirit consolidate as one within us.

> WE BECOME THE MANIFESTED SONS
> WHEN THE REVEALED WORD AND SPIRIT
> CONSOLIDATE AS ONE WITHIN US.

This was the point of empowerment for the Lord Jesus and the embodiment of the sevenfold Spirit of God to achieve His mandate and mission. It was at that point that the Spirit of the Lord came upon the Lord to demonstrate the spirits of wisdom and revelation, counsel and might, and knowledge and the reverential awe of God.

This reality is reiterated in Acts 10:38 where we are told:

> *How God anointed Jesus of Nazareth with the Holy Spirit and with power, who went about doing good and healing all who were oppressed by the devil, for God was with Him* (NKJV).

There was a specific anointing and empowerment to do the work of ministry. That same impartation will be made available to the bridal/son company to achieve the same mandate demonstrated by the Lord in His earthly ministry. We too must heal the sick, cast out devils, and even raise the dead by the same Spirit. This army will be "bone of His bone and flesh of His flesh."

TYPES AND SHADOWS

When plans for the construction of the Tabernacle were being communicated to Moses, he was instructed to make all things according to the heavenly pattern. They were to be a "copy and shadow of the heavenly things." One of the primary implements in the Holy Place was a lampstand burning with seven lamps. This was a foreshadowing representation of the Holy Spirit and His operation through people who become the Tabernacle of God. Paul emphasized in First Corinthians 3:16:

Do you not know that you are a temple of God and that the Spirit of God dwells in you?

Furthermore, the prophet Zechariah utilized incredible language to depict the workings of God's Spirit in the earth saying:

He said to me, "What do you see?" And I said, "I see, and behold, a lampstand all of gold with its bowl on the top of it, and its seven lamps on it with seven spouts belonging to each of the lamps which are on the top of it; also two olive trees by it, one on the right side of the bowl and the other on its left side." Then I said to the angel who was speaking with me saying, "What are these, my lord?" So the angel who was speaking with me answered and said to me, "Do you not know what these are?" And I said, "No, my lord." Then he said to me, "This is the word of the Lord to Zerubbabel saying, 'Not by might nor by power, but by My Spirit,' says the Lord of hosts" (Zechariah 4:2-6).

"These seven lamps" of fire burning as a single lampstand are the sevenfold Spirit of God. These are also the seven "*sent out into all the earth*" and the seven eyes of the Lord "*which range to and fro throughout the whole earth.*" This is an Old Testament portrayal of the seven eyes of God and the seven horns illustrated in the Book of Revelation. We glean further understanding of the sevenfold Spirit of God through John's visitation and description, saying:

> *And I saw between the throne* (with the four living creatures) *and the elders a Lamb standing, as if slain, having seven horns and seven eyes, which are the seven Spirits of God, sent out into all the earth* (Revelation 5:6).

John saw the Lord portrayed as a lamb with seven eyes and seven horns. This is another allegorical expression outlining what the Father was going to manifest through His son. Horns are symbolic representations of power or authority; seven is the number of completion. Therefore, we conclude that the Lord possessed complete and absolute revelation and power through the Holy Spirit in His earthly ministry.

LORD POSSESSED COMPLETE AND ABSOLUTE REVELATION AND POWER THROUGH THE HOLY SPIRIT IN HIS EARTHLY MINISTRY.

A REPRESENTATION OF GOD

The Seven Spirits of God are not merely attributes or spiritual manifestations but a perfect representation of God's Spirit—the sevenfold and flawless activity of the Holy Spirit carrying out and fulfilling Heaven's purposes in the earth. Likewise, the seven eyes illustrate unimpeded revelatory insight, not only accessing the Father's heart but also knowing the hearts of men. The Living Word is a discerner of the thoughts and intents of men's hearts as described in Hebrews 4:12.

For the Bride of Christ to do the works Jesus did and even greater works, we will also need the same manifestation of the Spirit in and through us. That is God's promise! There is a place of union with God that is so complete that He will express Himself through this company of people and do through them the same works He did while on the earth in human form. That is the revelation of the Kingdom.

It is clear that Isaiah 11:2 is a prophetic description of the Messiah and the spiritual empowerment that would identify His life and ministry. Jesus said as the Father sent Him, so also does He send us. If the Lord Jesus functioned in the sevenfold Spirit of God, then the Bride of Christ, when she reaches full maturity, will also function in this same manifestation of God! They are:

- The Spirit of the Lord
- The spirits of wisdom and understanding
- The spirits of counsel and might
- The spirits of knowledge and reverential awe of God

The spirits are placed in pairs because of the compatible nature of their functioning. I discussed the function of wisdom and revelation in the previous chapter. Here I would like to emphasize counsel and might.

COUNSEL AND MIGHT

Counsel is defined as advice, plans, or admonitions of prudence to provide leadership and proper decision-making to achieve God's plan and purpose. The term can be used to apply to secular or human counsel, but primarily counsel received from the Holy Spirit.

The Hebrew word for *counsel* is *etsah* and is used numerous times in the Old Testament and translated *counsel, advice, advisement,* or *purpose.* One of the first occurrences of the term is in Exodus 18:19, when Jethro gives counsel to Moses concerning the leadership of Israel.

According to Isaiah 9:6, the Lord Himself is known as the Wonderful Counselor. A counselor is one who gives advice or formulates a plan for the achievement of a specific goal. The spirit of counsel grants advice from God's throne and provides the perfect plan or strategy to achieve a specific mandate. The Lord does not merely have counsel; He is the spirit of counsel.

Might is taken from the Hebrew word *gebuwrah* and is defined as "power, strength, or force producing valor, victory, and mighty deeds." The spirit of might illustrates and demonstrates the marvelous acts and miraculous powers of the Holy Spirit. Deuteronomy 3:24 affirms this, saying:

*O Lord God, You have begun to show Your
servant Your greatness and Your strong hand;
for what god is there in heaven or on earth who
can do such works and mighty acts as Yours?*

These two spirits working in unison function through the Holy Spirit by giving advice or counsel, which formulates a plan that demonstrates the mighty acts and miraculous powers of God.

SPIRITUAL PROTOTYPES

When I first began to study the lives of several 20th-century leaders, I discovered there were a few who seemingly were set apart and functioned in this higher realm of power and authority. These included Maria Woodworth-Etter, John G. Lake, William Branham, and others. It seemed that each came to a specific juncture of their lives requiring total and complete surrender that catapulted them over into a different spiritual realm that characterized their greatest ministry. I believe they discovered the reality of Hebrews 6:5 and *"tasted the good word of God and the powers of the age to come."*

These ministries function as spiritual prototypes so that we can understand them and prepare to function as a bridal company in the same way. I remember specifically reading an incident that occurred in the ministry of William Branham that struck me as an incredible demonstration of the Spirit and a token of what is to come.

It occurred in the 1930s shortly after his ordination as a minister in the Baptist church. It started with a revelatory experience while in prayer, in which he seemingly found himself standing in a specific hospital room looking at a black man who had been run over by an automobile and pinned against the wheel of a wagon. The accident had severely injured the gentleman, causing many of his bones to be broken and severe damage to his internal organs. Some of the broken bones in his chest lay adjacent to his heart and lungs, which prohibited any movement for fear of certain death.

The prognosis was very grim. The minister found himself in the vision standing on one side of the bed looking at the man and understanding his medical condition. Furthermore, he watched as two white people came into the room and stood on the opposite side of the bed. At that moment he saw himself pronounce healing for the man who promptly leaped from the bed, dressed himself, and proceeded out of the hospital; then the vision ended.

A few days later, Branham discovered that the gentleman was indeed in the hospital in the exact condition he had seen in his vision. He took a friend to the hospital with him and told him to wait at the front of the hospital because very shortly a black man was going to walk out the front door wearing a very specific suit and carrying a plum hat.

Branham entered the hospital and found the room exactly as portrayed in the vision. There he found the gentleman just as he had seen him and entered to stand precisely where he had seen himself standing. However, he couldn't pray for the man until the two people came to stand on the opposite side of the bed as he had seen in the vision. While he stood there, the gentleman's wife shared the terrible prognosis and how the doctors had insisted upon immobilization or he would immediately die of internal injuries.

Finally, the two other people entered the room and stood on the other side of the bed. It turned out to be the people who were occupants of the car that accidentally ran over the man. When they entered, the man of God didn't just pray for healing; he announced it. It had already been accomplished in the vision. The moment prayer was offered, the man immediately responded by throwing back the covers and jumping out of bed and declaring, "I am healed."

Needless to say, the doctors and nurses were frantic to restrain the man for fear of immediate death. But the good news is he was completely healed. All his bones and organs were miraculously mended. He went to his closet, put on the clothes that had been seen in the vision, and walked out of the front of the hospital directly past brother Branham's friend, just as he had described that he would. This is a clear illustration of the operation of the spirits of counsel and might.

I especially enjoy this testimony because it was achieved just a generation ago. It is one thing to read the miraculous stories achieved in the ministries of Jesus, the

Old Testament prophets, or the early apostles. But it seems special and more readily attainable when demonstrated in the modern church era through ordinary people like us.

ADHERENCE TO COUNSEL RELEASED MIGHT

The word of counsel was to go to the room and wait for a specific set of circumstances to exist; the faithful adherence to the word of counsel released the spirit of might to produce a miracle. This is the same biblical model we see demonstrated in the ministry of the Lord Jesus as well as the Old Testament prophets who functioned in this spirit for a season.

> THE FAITHFUL ADHERENCE TO THE WORD OF COUNSEL RELEASED THE SPIRIT OF MIGHT TO PRODUCE A MIRACLE.

Naaman was instructed by the prophet Elisha to dip in the Jordan River seven times; his adherence to the word of counsel released the spirit of might to heal his leprosy. Jesus applied clay to a man's eyes and told him to go to a specific pool to wash the clay away; his meticulous obedience to the word of counsel released the spirit of might giving the man his sight. These are just a few of the many biblical illustrations outlining the function of the spirits of counsel and might.

Clearly, not every circumstance will be as vividly outlined as it was for Branham in his vision. Even so, whether received through prayer, the written Word, or prophetic utterance, our careful adherence to God's counsel releases the spirit of might to do awesome things.

THE LORD'S COUNSEL

In Revelation 3:18, the Lord gives us a word of counsel, saying:

> *I counsel you to buy from Me gold refined in the fire, that you may be rich; and white garments, that you may be clothed, that the shame of your nakedness may not be revealed; and anoint your eyes with eye salve, that you may see* (NKJV).

Our dedicated obedience to His counsel unleashes the empowerment to live the life of one who overcomes and is victorious over the spirit of this age. Thus, conquering spiritual opposition qualifies us to sit with Him on His throne as He overcame to sit with the Father. That is the heritage of those who have experienced the fullness of spiritual adoption and placed as mature sons in the Kingdom of our Father.

UNDERSTAND THE TRUTH ABOUT ADOPTION

The modern concept of adoption is a beautiful experience. The act of taking someone outside of your family and receiving them into your family and giving them the full rights and privileges as family members. What a beautiful expression of love! This concept of adoption has been in practice for many centuries. It was an integral part of the early Roman culture where individuals were received into a family and given birthright privileges as though directly born into the family.

However, the New Testament doctrine of "adoption" is not the same practice as we have understood it to be in our modern culture. The Greek term for *adoption* as used by the apostle Paul is *huiothesia*. It is the consolidation of two Greek words—*huious,* meaning "a mature man," and *thesis,* meaning "to place or set in position." Literally the term means "to place or set into position a mature son." It is not about becoming a son but the placing of a son into the fullness of his inheritance.

Very few people truly understand this extremely relevant concept, yet it is a vital last-day revelation that must be accurately comprehended and experienced for us to walk in the authority of sonship and fulfill the admonition of Paul in the Book of Romans. All of creation is groaning, waiting for the revelation of the mature sons of God who have been placed into their position and authority as sons. The term *huiothesia* is never a reference to the becoming of a son but the *placing* of a son. This has caused great confusion in the modern church. As a result, few people look at the spirit of adoption as a last-day mystery with great spiritual implications.

THE SEED OF GOD

An adopted child may partake of all the privileges of the family, yet they are not born into the family. Clearly, the

Scriptures tell us that we are from God's seed and have been begotten by our Father. We are not orphans who have been adopted into God's family. We are sons who have been birthed by the "*sperma*" of God. Therefore, we have the privilege to cry "Abba Father." First John 3:9 says:

> *No one who is born of God practices sin, because His seed abides in him; and he cannot sin, because he is born of God.*

This passage profoundly reiterates that God's seed *abides* within us. What a fantastic revelation. The Greek word for seed is *sperma,* meaning "something sown, a *seed* or by implication an offspring." It literally says we are the seed and offspring of God. Within that seed are God's invisible attributes, His divine nature, and His eternal power (see Rom. 1:20). This makes us the begotten of God and sons/daughters born of our Father. Therefore, the modern concept of adoption does not apply. The Complete Jewish Bible translates it this way, *"No one who has God as his Father keeps on sinning, because the seed planted by God remains in him. That is, he cannot continue sinning, because he has God as his Father."*

In the same way that our natural father's seed engenders us, so also are we born of the Spirit by our heavenly Father's seed. The DNA of our natural father is reflected in every cell of our body. So also is God's "seed" that abides within our spiritual constitution and defines who we are and provides God's potentials. As already stated, the modern practice of adoption is a beautiful practice. Even so, the adopted child does not receive the nature or DNA of their adoptive parents. When we are born again by God's seed, we are literally infused with the very nature of our heavenly Father.

> WHEN WE ARE BORN AGAIN BY GOD'S SEED, WE ARE LITERALLY INFUSED WITH THE VERY NATURE OF OUR HEAVENLY FATHER.

In the parable of the sower, the Lord tells us that the good seed/*sperma* are the sons of the Kingdom; the end of the age is the harvest when the sons will shine like the brightness of the sun in the Kingdom of our Father (see Matt. 13:24-43). That is where we are at the present hour. Harvest is the maturity of all seeds that have been sown.

Furthermore, First Peter 1:22-23 emphasizes essentially the same point, saying:

> *Since you have in obedience to the truth purified your souls for a sincere love of the brethren, fervently love one another from the heart, for you have been born again not of seed which is perishable but imperishable, that is, through the living and enduring word of God.*

We are born again by an imperishable seed/*sperma*. This is the source of our eternal life. Through faith in the resurrection of Jesus Christ, God took a little piece of Himself, which is eternal, and placed it within us to make us His offspring and heirs of promise. We are thereby born of His Spirit and possess the passions of Heaven that overcome the lusts of this world. The consolidation of Word and Spirit (in both men and women) always produces a mature son.

> GOD TOOK A LITTLE PIECE OF HIMSELF, WHICH IS ETERNAL, AND PLACED IT WITHIN US TO MAKE US HIS OFFSPRING AND HEIRS OF PROMISE.

God is eternal and He is Life. Therefore, what He placed within us provides eternal life in Him. As it states in the Scripture, we were in Christ before the foundation of the world. These last-day revelations are mandatory for us to fully appreciate the significance of sonship and the manifestation of God's dealings on planet Earth. We must be born of God's seed if we are to see the Kingdom of God (see John 3:3).

We are not born by accident nor are we orphans without spiritual heritage. We are born/begotten by the Spirit into the family of God by the living and enduring Word of God. God's seed abiding in us makes us His offspring! We receive an imperishable inheritance through God's imperishable seed (see 1 Pet. 1:3-4). He saw us before the foundation of the world, and by His foreknowledge predestined us to be in the image of His Son, that He would be the firstborn of many brethren (see Rom. 8:29-30). Selah! Think about the tremendous significance of that amazing truth. Yet, it is God's Word and must be achieved by this generation.

THE SPIRIT OF ADOPTION

The "spirit of adoption" is a powerful spiritual impartation that provokes us from infancy into adulthood. Romans 8:14-15 declares:

> *For all who are being led by the Spirit of God, these are sons* [huious] *of God. For you have not received a spirit of slavery leading to fear again, but you have received a spirit of adoption as sons by which we cry out, "Abba! Father!"*

Just as there is the spirit of faith, the spirit of revelation, the spirit of healing, so also is there the spirit of adoption as a meaningful deposit of the Holy Spirit that moves us from immaturity into the place of adulthood. When the spirit of adoption comes upon us, it is an impartation of grace that takes us from where we are to where we need to be in order for our full inheritance to be released. It is a provocation to grow and progress into a mature man. It is a literal fulfillment of Hebrews 6:1-5, moving from the elementary principles into the fullness of maturity.

> *Therefore leaving the elementary teaching about the Christ, let us press on to maturity, not laying again a foundation of repentance from dead works and of faith toward God, of instruction about washings and laying on of hands, and the resurrection of the dead and*

eternal judgment. And this we will do, if God permits. For in the case of those who have once been enlightened and have tasted of the heavenly gift and have been made partakers of the Holy Spirit, and have tasted the good word of God and the powers of the age to come.

In this passage we see four distinct progressions.

1. Once been enlightened—justification by faith

2. Tasted of the heavenly gift—sanctification by the washing of the water of the Word

3. Made partakers of the Holy Spirit—the baptism of the Holy Spirit

4. The tasting of the good Word of God and the powers of the age to come

It is this fourth and final progression that is of paramount importance as it relates to the mature sons of God in these last days. The model for what will be displayed in this hour cannot be found in the past but must be apprehended by revelation from the age to come. The mature sons who have experienced full adoption will demonstrate a firstfruits representation of the age to come. It will be an introduction to the new age as we culminate the present Church age. This is a fundamental aspect of the harvest.

> THE MODEL FOR WHAT WILL BE DISPLAYED
> IN THIS HOUR CANNOT BE FOUND IN
> THE PAST BUT MUST BE APPREHENDED BY
> REVELATION FROM THE AGE TO COME.

PAUL'S QUEST FOR ADOPTION

It is believed by many scholars that the apostle Paul wrote the Book of Romans from Corinth around A.D. 57. This would've been the end of Paul's third missionary journey. At the time, Rome was under the wicked leadership of Nero. Though the Church of Rome had been severely persecuted, it had persevered for many years with a strong core group of saints who were prepared to hear the deep truth that God revealed through Paul in this amazing Epistle.

By the time Paul penned Romans, he had been serving the Lord as an apostle for nearly twenty-five years and had endured great hardship for the sake of the Gospel. He had been imprisoned, stoned, beaten, shipwrecked, and persecuted; all this while birthing numerous churches and writing profound Epistles concerning church order and the great revelations that had been entrusted to him. Paul acknowledged that his revelation came not by the teaching of men nor by the reading of a book but by *"the revelation of Jesus Christ"* (Gal. 1:12)

Clearly, by the time he wrote Romans 8 he was a seasoned believer walking with the Lord for a quarter century. With that brief background in mind, let us now examine Romans 8:22-23 to understand more fully Paul's perspective on adoption, saying:

> *For we know that the whole creation groans and suffers the pains of childbirth together until now. And not only this, but also we ourselves, having the first fruits of the Spirit, even we ourselves groan within ourselves, waiting eagerly for our adoption as sons, the redemption of our body.*

Notice how Paul includes himself in this passage as he writes to veteran believers who have paid a great price for their walk with God. These are not people seeking to become believers but those who have been serving the Lord for many years. They were sealed into God by the Holy Spirit and possessed the firstfruits of the Spirit, including Paul himself. Yet he says, "We ourselves groan within ourselves, waiting eagerly for our adoption as sons."

This is a profound passage as it relates to the truth of spiritual adoption. Paul was not looking to the past to reflect on his new birth experience but rather looking to the future and his full adoption as a mature son with complete access to the fullness of his inheritance, including the redemption of his body. As such, no longer living according to the laws of sin and death but according to the laws of the Spirit of life in Christ Jesus. Redemption means to put back in its original order. Death is the result of sin. Once full adoption has been experienced, the curse and effects of the laws of sin and death have been entirely broken and the spirit of life prevails.

This places adoption as a last-day principle of the Spirit that must be understood for us to become the manifestation of God's sons who do the works Christ did and even greater works. Paul said he was groaning within himself, longing for his adoption. The word *groaning* is the Greek term *stenazo*, meaning "to sigh deep within, murmur or pray with groaning for something's reality." The very core of Paul's being cried out for his adoption (the setting in place) as a mature son. As we approach the end of this age, this truth will have even greater implications. The Bible tells us the end of the age is the harvest. The harvest implies that all things have come to maturity simultaneously. The sons of the Kingdom must come to a place of complete maturity to respond to the sons of the evil one as they come to the fullness of their maturity (see Matt. 13).

> THE SONS OF THE KINGDOM MUST COME TO A PLACE OF COMPLETE MATURITY TO RESPOND TO THE SONS OF THE EVIL ONE AS THEY COME TO THE FULLNESS OF THEIR MATURITY.

The orphan spirit must be broken in the Church through the revelation that we are the seed and offspring of the Living God. The spirit of adoption is now being released as a spiritual outpouring to rest upon those possessing God's seed/*sperma*. This provokes us into a deep walk with God, producing godly character and the expression of God's nature, thus accommodating the powers of the age to come.

We were chosen and foreknown by God before the foundation of the world to be perfected by the blood of Jesus Christ and presented holy and blameless. He predestined us for this purpose through the adoption as sons giving us complete access to our spiritual blessings in heavenly places. Ephesians 1:3-6 affirms this, saying:

> *Blessed be the God and Father of our Lord Jesus Christ, who has blessed us with every spiritual blessing in the heavenly places in Christ, just as He chose us in Him before the foundation of the world, that we would be holy and blameless before Him. In love He predestined us to adoption as sons through Jesus Christ to Himself, according to the kind intention of His will, to the praise of the glory of His grace, which He freely bestowed on us in the Beloved.*

COMING OF AGE

In ancient times when a wealthy man had a son born into his family who would ultimately become the heir of all he possessed, he would place that child under the training and supervision of guardians and tutors. The administrator was generally contracted by the father to guide, instruct, and even discipline a child to reflect the very image of the father. This process would continue until the time appointed by the father and full maturity had been reached. At that time, the child experienced adoption (was placed) as a mature son and given full rights and privileges of inheritance. He then could operate and conduct business on behalf of the father with the full approval and authority of his father. He was a son born of his father. That is the principle reflected in Galatians 4:1-5, saying:

> *Now I say, as long as the heir is a child, he does not differ at all from a slave although he is owner of everything, but he is under guardians and managers until the date set by the father. So also we, while we were children, were held in bondage under the elemental things of the world. But when the fullness of the time came, God sent forth His Son, born of a woman, born under the Law, so that He might redeem those who were under the Law, that we might receive the adoption as sons.*

Though the son is born with a right to everything within his father's household, he lives as a slave for a season until the time of maturity comes. One of the Greek words translated *son* in the New Testament is *teknon,* meaning a child still dependent upon his caretakers. Though that child has a right to everything, he has not yet reached the place of maturity to justify such a privilege. The time must come for him to become a *huious* son who has been trained and postured as a mature man. The adoption process is not the accepting of someone as a son but the placing of a son born into the family with full access to his inheritance.

> THE ADOPTION PROCESS IS NOT THE ACCEPTING OF SOMEONE AS A SON BUT THE PLACING OF A SON BORN INTO THE FAMILY WITH FULL ACCESS TO HIS INHERITANCE.

Ephesians 1 tells us that we are sealed into God by the Holy Spirit of promise as a pledge to the fullness of our inheritance (adoption). Paul, in writing Romans 8, addresses a community of people who had been sealed into God who already had the firstfruits of the Spirit but were longing and eagerly awaiting their adoption and the totality of their birthright. This is the hour for the manifestation of the mature sons in the fullness of the stature of Christ and the beautiful purified Bride that has made herself ready. Two sides of the same coin!

CHAPTER 4

THE BRIDE'S REVIVAL

WE ARE NOW entering a season of harvest and a time that will be known as the Bride's Revival. Church history has witnessed many expressions of outpouring and revival, but nothing like the days ahead when the Bride of Christ emerges in maturity and surrendered devotion to the Bridegroom.

Overall we are presently in the last-days' harvest, but it will come in multiple waves. The first harvest will be a harvest of harvesters, followed by a season of intense training and equipping. This was shown to me in vision form in 2003 at a time in which I witnessed the heavenly release of the "Angels That Gather" (see Matt. 13:41). Following that, the greatest harvest of souls throughout the earth will transpire in the Bride's Revival.

Those individuals who have yielded to the preparation process will experience the transformation of their perceived wilderness into a flourishing garden with pools of spiritual water. For them, a season of breakthrough will be accomplished that makes them a spiritual habitation of God's presence and the sevenfold Spirit of God.

> THOSE INDIVIDUALS WHO HAVE YIELDED TO THE PREPARATION PROCESS WILL EXPERIENCE THE TRANSFORMATION OF THEIR PERCEIVED WILDERNESS INTO A FLOURISHING GARDEN WITH POOLS OF SPIRITUAL WATER.

In essence, there will be a deposit of the "spirit to overcome" delegated to believers who have yielded their hearts and souls with unwavering desperation for the person of Jesus; that is what it means to be the Joshua generation. The Joshua commission is the anointing to "overcome." Heaven's empowerment will be granted to experience individual breakthrough. This grace will allow us to plant spiritual fields and vineyards that will produce bountiful harvests.

OPENING HEAVEN'S ARMORY

Jeremiah prophesied that:

> *The Lord has opened His armory and has brought forth the weapons of His indignation, for it is a work of the Lord God of hosts in the land of the Chaldeans* (Jeremiah 50:25).

Heaven's "storehouse," to which we are now given greater access, is a prophetic portrayal of the divinely powerful weapons that have been provided for us through Christ's sufferings and, more importantly, His resurrection. It is resurrection life that He desires to delegate. In this spiritual armory are "mantles" of spiritual authority and power as well as great ministries of healing and creative miracles that will result in restored limbs and organs.

Days of divine visitation are clearly marked with the miraculous. The latter rain revival that was initiated in 1946 is remembered as one of the most significant expressions of God's miracle working power recorded in modern church history. Many historians say it was the greatest outpouring of power since the early church.

The last 120 years of spiritual activity have functioned in the order of Moses. Clearly, Moses was one of the greatest men of God who ever lived. His intimate friendship with the Lord set a standard we aspire to today. Even so, the totality of his original mandate was not fully achieved in his lifetime. The Lord put the Spirit that rested on Moses onto Joshua, who then carried the people into the promise.

Moses brought the people out of Egypt under God's mighty hand of power through miracles, signs, and wonders; but that generation did not cross over into their destiny because of their "stiff-necked" condition. According to Deuteronomy 29:2-4, they did not possess the revelatory anointing essential to cooperate with God. Moses admonished them, saying:

> *You have seen all that the Lord did before your*
> *eyes in the land of Egypt to Pharaoh and all*

his servants and all his land; the great trials which your eyes have seen, those great signs and wonders. Yet to this day the Lord has not given you a heart to know, nor eyes to see, nor ears to hear.

Their eyes and ears were not opened and their hearts were not devoted to the revelation of Heaven's plan. As a result, they were disqualified and a season of discipline ensued.

Nevertheless, the next generation under Joshua's leadership emerged with spiritual hunger and desperation that captured Heaven's attention and positioned them for their inheritance. That is the same model we have followed over the last century.

It Is the Gift of God

The Bible clearly outlines that every good and perfect gift comes from the Father of Lights. God is Light and in Him there is no shifting shadow. Consequently, we are likewise called to be light in the midst of this dark generation.

It was by His own will that he gave us birth as "sons of the Kingdom" and the "Bride of Christ" by His Word of Truth; these two callings are two sides of the same coin. We are designated to be a form of firstfruits of His creation and a representation of what the "sons of the Kingdom" are called and consecrated to be.

Through his Epistle to the Ephesians, the apostle Paul exhorts us to conduct ourselves as children of light. He said:

Therefore do not be partakers with them; for
you were formerly darkness, but now you are
Light in the Lord; walk as children of Light (for
the fruit of the Light consists in all goodness
and righteousness and truth), trying to learn
what is pleasing to the Lord (Ephesians 5:7-10).

The surest evidence of the "children of Light" and the Bride of the Bridegroom will be the clear presence of the fruit of the Spirit. This place in God qualifies us for the supernatural endowments of the Seven Spirits of God and empowers us for the harvest.

> THE SUREST EVIDENCE OF THE
> "CHILDREN OF LIGHT" AND THE BRIDE
> OF THE BRIDEGROOM WILL BE THE CLEAR
> PRESENCE OF THE FRUIT OF THE SPIRIT.

God's righteousness will begin to reflect the Spirit's nature in our lives. The display of His character in us is ultimately pleasing to the Lord and the reflection of His Light that we must possess.

MARKED BY HEAVEN

The biblical mark of the "sons of the Kingdom" and the "Bride of Christ" is highlighted in Matthew 13:

The one who sows the good seed is the Son of
Man, and the field is the world; and as for the
good seed, these are the sons of the kingdom...

the harvest is the end of the age; and the reapers are angels (Matthew 13:37-39).

If we are to function as the Bride of Christ and the "light" of the world, we will possess qualities consistent with the Bridegroom and children of light by allowing Christ to be fully manifested in us. The identification, anointing, and purpose of this company who overcomes are listed below.

Their Identification

The manifestation of the fruit of the Spirit is found in Galatians 5:22-24:

1. Love
2. Joy
3. Peace
4. Patience
5. Kindness
6. Goodness
7. Faithfulness
8. Gentleness
9. Self-Control

Their Anointing

The Seven Spirits of God seen in Isaiah 11:2:

1. Spirit of the Lord
2. Spirit of Wisdom

3. Spirit of Understanding

4. Spirit of Counsel

5. Spirit of Might

6. Spirit of Knowledge

7. Spirit of Reverential Fear of the Lord

Their Purpose

To reveal the twelve names illustrating the divine character of God and His primary redemptive attributes manifested in the Person of Jesus:

1. Lord Our Shepherd

2. Lord Our Provider

3. Lord Our Righteousness

4. Lord Our Peace

5. Lord Our Healer

6. Lord Our Banner

7. Lord Who Sanctifies

8. Lord of Hosts

9. Lord Most High

10. Lord Who Smites

11. Lord of Recompense

12. Lord Is Present

OUR MANDATE

The prophet Ezekiel was taken to a valley of dry bones. He was not instructed to condemn them but to prophesy life to them. He said:

> *I prophesied as He commanded me, and the breath came into them, and they came to life and stood on their feet, an exceedingly great army. Then He said to me, "Son of man, these bones are the whole house of Israel; behold, they say, 'Our bones are dried up and our hope has perished. We are completely cut off.' Therefore prophesy and say to them, 'Thus says the Lord God, "Behold, I will open your graves and cause you to come up out of your graves, My people; and I will bring you into the land of Israel."'"* (Ezekiel 37:10-12)

That is our hope and expectation. We desire to breathe life into dry bones and begin to see them take shape and form a troop of those who overcome.

> WE DESIRE TO BREATHE LIFE INTO DRY BONES AND BEGIN TO SEE THEM TAKE SHAPE AND FORM A TROOP OF THOSE WHO OVERCOME.

Though the western Church may look like a valley of dry bones, I believe the Lord sees her prophetically as an exceedingly great army. We are convinced our nation and the western Church has an incredible destiny yet to be fulfilled as a leader among nations to introduce the Bride's Revival globally. When people are given a glimpse of their individual role in that destiny, it transforms them and sets them on the course to repentance and the impartation of the Christlike nature.

They see the cause of God and are forever changed and have the joy of their salvation restored. We are seeing that happen now. Strongholds of hopelessness, despair, depression, and other oppressive mind-sets will be overcome when God's *zoe* life is breathed into this army and it begins to functions as the Bride of the Bridegroom.

CHAPTER 5

THOSE WITH INSIGHT WILL UNDERSTAND

As I HAVE traveled the US, Canada, and abroad, I have noticed one consistent theme throughout the Body of Christ involving those who are earnestly contending for the faith that was once delivered to the saints; they have been through notable trials, tribulations, and refinements. Clearly, we are living in the days foreseen by the prophet Daniel when he was told:

> *Go your way, Daniel, for these words are concealed and sealed up until the end time. Many will be purged, purified and refined, but the wicked will act wickedly; and none of the wicked will understand, but those who have insight will understand* (Daniel 12:9-10).

Many of God's people have known firsthand the purging, purifying, and refining process. Possessing understanding of God's ways is of vital importance and will be a major dividing line between those who are fruitful and those who have the seed of the Kingdom stolen from them (see Matt. 13:19-23). The Scripture tells us that many of God's people perish for lack of knowledge and comprehension of the times. Nevertheless, great understanding is being released that will catapult a body of people into notable fruitfulness.

> GREAT UNDERSTANDING IS BEING RELEASED THAT WILL CATAPULT A BODY OF PEOPLE INTO NOTABLE FRUITFULNESS.

I remember the early days when I first realized that God still deals with His people in all the same ways outlined in the Bible and how excited I was to discover the ministry of Kenneth Hagin. One of the first of his books that I read that greatly impacted my life was *I Believe in Visions.*

To this day I am still contending for the fullness of what the Lord used that book to impart into my life. Through Dad Hagin, I learned the message of supernatural faith, living a life in the miraculous, our promise of divine health, and overcoming the schemes of the adversary. Even so, it is undeniable that many of God's choice soldiers who live in realms of radical faith have been through extreme conditioning, refinements, and pruning that have been somewhat difficult to interpret.

This, however, has been for a good cause. Though it is difficult to reconcile this process with our belief in the abundant life as taught by the "faith movement," many are about to emerge from this refinement with divine character and a clear vision of God's end-time plan because of these dealings. They will be called the Bride of Christ, and there will be a very specific anointing that will characterize their lives and ministries.

I believe this company of people will be synonymous with those described in Revelation 2 and 3 as those who "overcome." "To him who overcomes" is a notable phrase with substantial spiritual benefits and blessings. They include:

1. To eat from the tree of life in the paradise of God

2. To not be hurt by the second death

3. To eat of the hidden manna and receive a new name written on a white stone

4. To rule the nations with a rod of iron and receive the morning star

5. To be clothed in white garments, and He will not blot out his name from the Book of Life; but the Lord will confess his name before the Father and before His angels

6. To become a pillar in the temple of god and the name new Jerusalem

7. To sit with the Lord on His throne as He overcame to sit with the Father

VICTORIOUS ONES

In the Greek language, the expression "to overcome" means "to be victorious." Presently, there are a number of people emerging as "victorious ones," having overcome diverse circumstances that have trained and developed their character. Many of the generals of the faith throughout biblical history discovered a higher place in God through their trials.

> MANY OF THE GENERALS OF THE FAITH THROUGHOUT BIBLICAL HISTORY DISCOVERED A HIGHER PLACE IN GOD THROUGH THEIR TRIALS.

Clearly, David found faith and rest in God during the season Saul attempted to abort his opportunity to rule. The three Hebrew children discovered the Lord in the fiery furnace and emerged totally set free from all bondage. Daniel embraced God's protection and sovereignty in the lion's den. Moses experienced God's rest in his forty-year training season while tending sheep. Peter was sifted like wheat in order to emerge with the level of character needed to preach on the day of Pentecost one of the greatest sermons ever delivered.

The list could go on and on. It is not our intent to prophesy more trials and tribulations, but the emergence of a company of people from them into a place of significant anointing and authority. The fact that many have been in this process is undeniable, but we need the understanding that this has been part of the qualification, not disqualification as our accuser would like for us to believe.

Daniel prophesied this would take place resulting in a body of people with considerable insight who had understanding of God's ways and God's relevant times and seasons. That is what we are fervently contending for. The spirit of understanding is being released to a company of people who emerge with authentic spiritual authority and power in order to facilitate the harvest.

Many are genuinely being baptized in the Holy Ghost and *fire* that consumes the chaff of selfish ambition, human striving, and improper motives. The God who desires to fill us and abide in us is a consuming fire and a jealous God. He wants all of us! Revelation 5:6 declares:

> *And I saw between the throne (with the four living creatures) and the elders a Lamb standing, as if slain, having seven horns and seven eyes, which are the seven Spirits of God, sent out into all the earth.*

The One who walks among the lampstands has perfect revelatory insight to see the issues standing against our highest calling. God's desire is for our personal enlightenment to see ourselves from His perspective. In so doing, we are on the journey for victory and the activation of our destiny.

SEVENFOLD SPIRIT OF GOD

I have addressed the impartation of the sevenfold Spirit of God promised to this Bridal Company called to do the "greater works." Isaiah 11:1-2 declares:

> *Then a shoot will spring from the stem of Jesse, and a branch from his roots will bear fruit. The Spirit of the Lord will rest on Him, the spirit of wisdom and understanding, the spirit of counsel and strength, the spirit of knowledge and the fear of the Lord.*

Jesus prophesied that as He was sent so shall we be sent to do the works He did. We have already outlined the basic functioning of the spirits of wisdom and understanding and counsel and might, and we will now seek to more fundamentally understand the spirits of knowledge and reverential fear of God.

THE SPIRITS OF KNOWLEDGE AND REVERENTIAL FEAR

As with the other spirits outlined in Isaiah 11:2, the spirits of knowledge and reverential fear of the Lord work in unison, seemingly in a "cause and effect" function. We see this demonstration clearly outlined in John 1 involving Nathaniel's encounter with the Lord Jesus.

In the process of choosing His disciples, the Lord journeyed to the region of Galilee and found Philip and commissioned him as a disciple. Philip in turn went to his friend Nathaniel and shared with him his enthusiastic encounter with Jesus. Nathaniel responded rather apathetically, saying, "Can anything good come out of Nazareth?" Philip wisely responded by encouraging him to see for himself.

While Nathaniel was yet approaching Him, the Lord said, "Behold, an Israelite indeed, in whom there is no guile!" As the exchange continued, Nathaniel was somewhat puzzled by this response and asked the Lord how He knew of his character. The Lord said, "Before Philip called you, when you were under the fig tree, I saw you." That single expression involving supernatural insight provided by the spirit of knowledge provoked Nathaniel through the awe-inspiring nature of God and he responded saying, "Rabbi, You are the Son of God! You are the king of Israel!"

That response was quite a distinction from his earlier perception! Clearly there was a spiritual atmosphere that surrounded this encounter that pierced Nathaniel's heart, provoking him to awe-inspiring faith that changed the remainder of his life. This is the functioning of the spirits of knowledge and reverential awe.

KNOWLEDGE AND REVERENTIAL FEAR: VITAL TO THE LAST DAYS

Spirit of knowledge is taken from the Hebrew word *da'ath* and could be defined as "spiritually imparted knowledge, skill, awareness, comprehension, and discernment that are conveyed as instruction and insight from God's heart and sovereignty."

Spirit of reverential fear is taken from the Hebrew word *yir'ah,* meaning "awe-inspiring, terrible, and awesome." Reverential fear in its purest form is birthed out of love. We fear/revere God because we love Him and have a revelatory knowledge of His nature and character! It is a working of the Holy Spirit that produces a reverential fear of God. The fear of the Lord does not make us afraid of God, but instead catapults our faith into the supernatural realm through a revelation of how great He truly is.

> THE FEAR OF THE LORD DOES NOT MAKE US AFRAID OF GOD, BUT INSTEAD CATAPULTS OUR FAITH INTO THE SUPERNATURAL REALM THROUGH A REVELATION OF HOW GREAT HE TRULY IS.

These two spirits functioning in unison constitute the working of the Holy Spirit that imparts a comprehension from God with ability to discern the hearts of men and diverse situations. Its consequence is a wholesome and reverential awe of God. Knowledge and reverential fear open the spiritual realm and enlighten our eyes of understanding to look unto God. This produces a healthy and overwhelming reverence for God's character that promotes intimate relationship and abundant spiritual blessings.

SECRETS OF THE HEART REVEALED

This same principle is also outlined in First Corinthians 14:24-25:

But if all prophesy, and an unbeliever or an uninformed person comes in, he is convinced by all, he is convicted by all. And thus the secrets of his heart are revealed; and so, falling down on his face, he will worship God and report that God is truly among you (NKJV).

In this passage, the apostle Paul is describing how supernaturally imparted secrets of the heart produce awe-inspiring results. I have actually seen this concept in operation when the Holy Spirit is powerfully present to reveal knowledge and information about a person's life that the individual ministering had no natural way of knowing. This always produces the same result Paul describes in this passage. The people will acknowledge that God is present and doing awesome things. It is then up to the individual to make the decision to accept or reject the grace God is offering.

As I have studied church history and in particular what has been known as the voice of healin revival, I noticed numerous occasions when this principle operated and produced tremendous outcomes. I have actually interviewed a number of individuals who attended those meetings in the '50s and '60s. I have often asked what it was like to be in an atmosphere when the manifest Presence of God was present to reveal individuals' names, addresses, secret desires, personal needs, and other information known only to God.

Invariably, the response is consistently the same—they all said the fear of the Lord was so manifestly present that it felt tangible and the attitude prevailed that anything was possible in this super charged atmosphere.

How desperately we need to return to those blessings and function in God's sevenfold Spirit producing these results. History records countless millions who were saved through that revival and multiplied thousands of others supernaturally healed and delivered of the most heinous infirmities. The pathway to this reality can be discovered through embracing our refining and grooming process. We then emerge with the character and compassion to be entrusted with the "secret of the Lord" and divine information to be administered in wholesome ways. This ultimately produces an atmosphere of reverential awe.

Psalm 25:12-14 declares:

Who is the man that fears the Lord? Him shall He teach in the way He chooses. He himself shall dwell in prosperity, and his descendants shall inherit the earth. The secret of the Lord is with those who fear Him, and He will show them His covenant (NKJV).

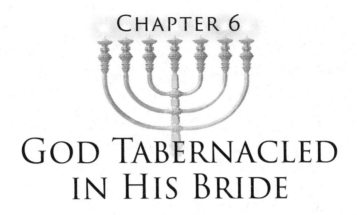

CHAPTER 6

GOD TABERNACLED
IN HIS BRIDE

THROUGHOUT THE BODY of Christ, one word is consistently accentuated to identify our present place in church history—*transition*. I wrote extensively about this subject in my book *Angels That Gather*.

As time progresses, greater clarity is coming into view as to the nature of this shift and how the Bride of Christ should position herself. Clearly, we are thankful for every expression of spiritual outpouring enjoyed in recent years. However, we also recognize these "revivals" have not yet fulfilled what has been promised for this age nor what we as the Ekklesia have been contending for.

There is something uniquely woven into the spiritual DNA of an overcoming generation that desperately longs for the invisible union of the heavenly Bridegroom and the earthly Bride. This "revival" will take on different characteristics from any previously demonstrated in church history. It will be distinguished by passion and purity paving the way for more pronounced expressions of power and authority; it will be the Lord Himself fully "tabernacled" in His people.

> THERE IS SOMETHING UNIQUELY WOVEN INTO THE SPIRITUAL DNA OF AN OVERCOMING GENERATION THAT DESPERATELY LONGS FOR THE INVISIBLE UNION OF THE HEAVENLY BRIDEGROOM AND THE EARTHLY BRIDE.

This transition can easily be identified with a historically important time for the nation of Israel and their commitment to worship the God of Abraham, Isaac, and Jacob. The Feast of Tabernacles was the final feast of the seventh month symbolizing this present season. Prophetically it is known as:

- The Feast of the Open Book
- The Feast of Rest
- The Feast of Glory
- The Feast of Restoration
- The Feast of His Appearing
- The Feast of Ingathering

With the closing of the harvest year, centered on the ingathering of fruit, the Israelites set aside a time of rejoicing and celebration. According to the Lord's instructions, they were to leave their homes and construct temporary booths in which they resided as a prophetic picture of the

Lord Himself dwelling for a short season within His people before he comes to permanently reside in the millennial Kingdom. The "booths" symbolized temporary dwelling places to be occupied en route to the Promised Land.

The Lord spoke to me extensively in 1994 about the importance of Tabernacles in the midst of an extended fast. Now, years later, I am seeing many of the things spoken at that time poised for fulfillment.

THREE TIMES A YEAR

Three times a year the Israelites were required to gather in Jerusalem to observe the feasts of the Lord. These were called *moeds* or divine appointments. Passover, Pentecost, and Tabernacles were each built around the harvest cycles. In them there is considerable prophetic insight to help identify where we are in history and what God's people ought to do.

> *Also you shall observe the Feast of the Harvest of the first fruits of your labors from what you sow in the field; also the Feast of the Ingathering at the end of the year when you gather in the fruit of your labors from the field. Three times a year all your males shall appear before the Lord God* (Exodus 23:16-17).

The Feast of the First Month—Passover

1. The Feast of Passover
2. The Feast of Unleavened Bread
3. The Feast of Firstfruits

The Feast of the Third Month—Pentecost

1. The Feast of Weeks

The Feast of the Seventh Month—Tabernacles

1. The Feast of Trumpets
2. The Feast Day of Atonement
3. The Feast of Tabernacles

APPLICATION OF THE BLOOD

1. In Passover the blood was sprinkled upon the door.
2. In Pentecost the blood was sprinkled on the people and the covenant book.
3. In Tabernacles the blood was sprinkled seven times on the mercy seat.

SPIRITUAL ISRAEL

Clearly, the Lord's Church is spiritual Israel. What happened to natural Israel historically provides types and shadows of what is to take place during the Church age. First the natural then the spiritual—the apostle made this profoundly clear in First Corinthians 10:11 and First Corinthians 15:46, saying:

> *Now all these things happened to them [Israel] as examples, and they were written for our admonition, upon whom the ends of the ages have come* (NKJV).

However, the spiritual is not first, but the natural, and afterward the spiritual (NKJV).

Each of the three feasts must also be experientially revealed in and through God's people. There is an abundance of historical evidence from the New Testament that affirms two of the three annual feasts of the Lord have been fulfilled in Christ and His Church. We now stand on the brink of the fulfillment of the last feast that will usher in the Lord's return. This is the feast of the seventh month or the Feasts of Ingathering—Tabernacles.

END-OF-THE-AGE HARVEST

We live in the days of the final harvest. Jesus said the end of the age is the harvest, and during that season He would send "angels that gather" all stumbling blocks and everything offensive out of His Kingdom so that the righteous would shine like the sun in the Kingdom of our Father (see Matt. 13:41,43). This will be the unveiling of the Sons of God who will exhibit a power and glory not yet seen in church history.

It will be the Lord Jesus "tabernacled" in His Bride to demonstrate His Kingdom and His divine nature. There are ever increasing heights of truth and glory that are to be appropriated in these last days. It is upon this prize that we fix our hopes and expectations for the full revelation of who He is and what He is able to do through us as a result of the Cross.

The Feast of Tabernacles is also known as the Feast of Rest. This is the promised rest spoken of in Hebrews, saying:

> *For if Joshua had given them rest, He would not have spoken of another day after that. So there remains a Sabbath rest for the people of God. For the one who has entered His rest has himself also rested from his works, as God did from His. Therefore let us be diligent to enter that rest, so that no one will fall, through following the same example of disobedience* (Hebrews 4:8-11).

The Spirit's anointing that came upon the Old Testament prophets rested for a season until God's mandate was complete and then it lifted; in the ministry of the Lord Jesus the Spirit remained and "tabernacled" in the Son of God. The Bible declares that the heavens opened and the Holy Spirit descended as the appearance of a dove *and remained* (see John 1:32). This is our promise as well; just as He was sent so also will we be sent!

WE WISH TO SEE JESUS

An interesting exchange took place in John 12:20-24 with fascinating implications for this day. Two of His disciples informed the Lord that a company of Greeks had come with a request, saying, "Sir, we wish to see Jesus." The Lord's reply seemed odd unless you read it from a contemporary point of view understanding the incredible prophetic implications of His statement. He said:

The hour has come for the Son of Man to be glorified. Truly, truly, I say to you, unless a grain of wheat falls into the earth and dies, it remains alone; but if it dies, it bears much fruit (John 12:23-24).

The Lord Himself was the grain of wheat that went into the earth. That Seed has experienced two thousand years of growth, pruning, and maturation, until at the end of the age there will be an ingathering harvest of exponentially multiplied grains of wheat just like the original seed. That is the principal outlined in Genesis 1:11-12—seed produces after its own kind. This last-days' generation is saying, "We wish to see Jesus," and that is to occur in His Bride/sons as a seed harvest like the original that went into the earth.

> ## THIS LAST-DAYS' GENERATION IS SAYING, "WE WISH TO SEE JESUS."

The Lord prophesied in Matthew 13 that the end of the age will be the harvest and the wheat sown into the earth as "sons of the Kingdom." This reality can only be achieved when the Lord's Spirit is fully manifested and abiding within His sons/bridal company doing the greater works. Then this generation will "see Jesus" in a real and tangible way. This will bring in the fullness of the Gentiles as promised by the apostle Paul in Romans 11.

LEAVEN-FREE

When the Lord discovers His rest in us, we will then discover our promised rest from the toils and labors that make us weary emotionally and spiritually. It is in this season that we will be most fruitful. The Feast of Pentecost allowed the use of leaven. Leaven is a symbol of false teachings, religiosity, and mixture. The Pentecostal age witnessed much "leaven" woven throughout. However, the day has come for the remnant of God's people to be leaven free. The Lord once said, "If I can find a people without mixture, I will release My Spirit without measure." That is what lies imminently before us.

> WHEN THE LORD DISCOVERS HIS REST IN US WE WILL THEN DISCOVER OUR PROMISED REST FROM THE TOILS AND LABORS THAT MAKE US WEARY EMOTIONALLY AND SPIRITUALLY.

The Feast of Tabernacles included trumpets as a prophetic picture calling for a holy convocation and preparation for purification and cleansing. The day of atonement and ingathering prophetically set forth the final operation of the Lord in the earth prior to His second coming.

The final harvest of souls before the Lord's return will then be facilitated. It sets in motion the gatherings or calling out of the saints unto the Lord and the perfection of the Church by the power of blood atonement. That is, we are to know the full measure of redemption and the power of His atonement, thereby fulfilling the apostle Paul's prayer:

> *Now may the God of peace Himself sanctify you entirely; and may your spirit and soul and body be preserved complete, without blame at the coming of our Lord Jesus Christ* (1 Thessalonians 5:23).

The fullness of the feast of the seventh month overflows or overlaps into the seventh day of the Lord, which is the Kingdom age to be enjoyed for one thousand years.

SANCTIFIED IN TRUTH

When Moses was 120 years of age, he passed the torch to Joshua along with a renewal of the covenant for the new generation born in the wilderness. And he said to them:

> *I am a hundred and twenty years old today; I am no longer able to come and go, and the Lord has said to me, "You shall not cross this Jordan." It is the Lord your God who will cross ahead of you; He will destroy these nations before you, and you shall dispossess them. Joshua is the one who will cross ahead of you, just as the Lord has spoken* (Deuteronomy 31:2-3).

A new command was given to the Joshua generation. God's priests were to take the Book of the Covenant and open it during the Feast of Tabernacles when entering the Land of Promise. Israel experienced Pentecost in the wilderness but Tabernacles in the Land of Promise.

> *So Moses wrote this law and gave it to the priests, the sons of Levi who carried the ark of the covenant of the Lord, and to all the elders of Israel. Then Moses commanded them, saying, "At the end of every seven years, at the time of the year of remission of debts, at the Feast of Booths, when all Israel comes to appear before the Lord your God at the place which He will choose, you shall read this law in front of all Israel in their hearing. Assemble the people, the men and the women and children and the alien who is in your town, so that they may hear and learn and fear the Lord your God, and be careful to observe all the words of this law. Their children, who have not known, will hear and learn to fear the Lord your God, as long as you live on the land which you are about to cross the Jordan to possess"* (Deuteronomy 31:9-13).

Not in Passover nor in Pentecost, but in Tabernacles was the book opened and revealed before all the people. This is a picture of the mysteries of the Kingdom being unveiled to provide insight and illumination to cause us to:

> *Shine brightly like the brightness of the expanse of heaven, and those who lead the many to*

righteousness, like the stars forever and ever (Daniel 12:3).

Furthermore, great Kingdom mysteries were revealed to Daniel but concealed in a book until the end-of-time generation. These prophecies of Daniel likewise clearly point to this season of history when the book that had been previously concealed at the Lord's instruction is now opened and devoured by a bridal company at the end of time, when many will go back and forth and knowledge will increase. It is at this time that we fulfill the prophetic directive of Revelation 10:11. The Lord is manifesting Himself in the Earth with feet "like pillars of fire," placing them on the land and sea. He is beckoning us to take the now opened book from His hand, consume it, and *"prophesy again concerning many peoples and nations and tongues and kings."*

As the end-of-time generation experiences the fullness of the Feast of Tabernacles, there will be accelerated light and illumination delegated to us as full and complete truth is unveiled. Then:

1. We will shine like the brightness of the sun in the Kingdom of our Father (see Matt. 13:43).

2. We will shine like the brightness of the expanse of Heaven and lead many to righteousness (see Dan. 12:3).

3. We will arise and shine for our light has come, though darkness covers the earth and deep darkness the people, the glory of the Lord will be revealed through His people (see Isa. 60:1-2).

4. Then you will see and become radiant and your heart will tremble and be enlarged (see Isa. 60:5).

The Feast of Tabernacles is the Feast of the Open Book with the delegated responsibility to the royal priesthood to teach the fullness of God's Kingdom and the mysteries and secrets reserved for the last-days' generation. This presents the Bride without spot or wrinkle.

Spiritual truth was revealed at Passover and Pentecost, but in Tabernacles full and complete truth will come into the Bride of Christ making her a bright, shining light to the nations. This will ultimately prepare her for the Lord and:

Sanctify her, having cleansed her by the washing of water with the word, that He might present to Himself the church in all her glory, having no spot or wrinkle or any such thing; but that she would be holy and blameless (Ephesians 5:26-27).

CHAPTER 7

FIRSTFRUITS BRIDAL COMPANY

IN HIS CLASSIC book *The Pursuit of God*, A.W. Tozer wrote, "The simplicity which is in Christ is rarely found among us. In its stead are programs, methods, organizations and a world of nervous activities which occupy time and attention but can never satisfy the longing of the heart."

Although this objective appraisal was written a generation ago, its truth is still pertinent to our day. Even so, hidden among us there exists a company of people who will never be satisfied substituting religious activities for intimacy with Christ and the fullness of His stature.

> EVEN SO, HIDDEN AMONG US THERE EXISTS A COMPANY OF PEOPLE WHO WILL NEVER BE SATISFIED SUBSTITUTING RELIGIOUS ACTIVITIES FOR INTIMACY WITH CHRIST AND THE FULLNESS OF HIS STATURE.

For a season, God concealed David in the Cave of Adullam. At the appropriate time, he and his mighty band emerged in strength to execute God's commission. So shall it be with this company. In this hour, many who have been hidden will suddenly break through from relative obscurity to the forefront as a token representation of a hidden company prepared until God's appointed timing. The moment of this spiritual confrontation is not yet certain; perhaps the praying Church will ultimately determine that. But one thing is clear—God knows how to groom and release champions who embrace and embody righteous standards of leadership.

Many who are called to play key leadership roles in the Bride's preparation are not even widely known on earth; but they are recognized in Heaven. They are spiritual warriors who have received God's imputed righteousness and carry His influence. Having captured Heaven's attention, it is now time to arise like Moses from the wilderness and shine like a bright evening star. Only then are we qualified to exercise the Lord's delegated authority to usher in a wave of harvest. Daniel foretold that:

> *Those who have insight will shine brightly like the brightness of the expanse of heaven, and those who lead the many to righteousness, like the stars forever and ever* (Daniel 12:3).

We are presently called to a heightened place of intimacy and fellowship with God. Our covenant is built upon better promises than that of Moses. Even so, Moses was required to veil his face because of the residue of God's glory resulting from his close encounter with Him. How much more should we experience His glory in the new covenant and the literal fulfillment of the spiritual implications associated with the Feast of Tabernacles!

NEW SEVEN-YEAR CYCLE

In many ways, 2021 ushered in a new seven-year season in God; it will be much different from the previous seven-year cycle that emphasized warfare and preparation. Substantial fruitfulness and restoration will characterize those who are spiritually mature and strengthened to become trustworthy stewards of His mysteries and power. A firstfruits company will begin to experience heavenly realms and embrace great insights from the now "opened book" containing notable strategies and revelations of the Lord (see Rev. 10).

> SUBSTANTIAL FRUITFULNESS AND RESTORATION WILL CHARACTERIZE THOSE WHO ARE SPIRITUALLY MATURE AND STRENGTHENED TO BECOME TRUSTWORTHY STEWARDS OF HIS MYSTERIES AND POWER.

There is a present and preparatory word being released in God's people essential for the impending outpouring. It is through His Word abiding in us merged with the Spirit that makes us "sons of the Kingdom" and the "Tabernacle of God." To espouse man-made traditions, doctrines, and perceptions of men rather than the true revelation of the Word will only become a cumbersome weight that interferes with our ability to meet the challenges of this new day.

> *Therefore gird up the loins of your mind, be sober, and rest your hope fully upon the grace that is to be brought to you at the revelation of Jesus Christ* (1 Peter 1:13 NKJV).

For years, the Lord has been nurturing and empowering many people in anticipation of this hour. We are now at a crossroad in His blueprint with great change on the horizon. As we determine to worship the Lord in spirit and truth, we will also draw nearer to His heart with greater levels of revelatory insight. This model is essential to be entrusted with keys to the Kingdom that unlock Heaven's greatest resources.

DEEP TO DEEP

This group, by responding to "deep calling unto deep," has been prepared to travel in a new way not yet known to the Church. Our call is to be equipped to carry mantles of power that will be unique to the harvest generation. The spirit of prophecy will call these things forth. According to Isaiah 48:6-7:

> *You have heard [these things foretold], now you see this fulfillment. And will you not bear witness to it? I show you specified new things from this time forth, even hidden things [kept in reserve] which you have not known. They are*

created now [called into being by the prophetic word], and not long ago; and before today you have never heard of them, lest you should say, Behold, I knew them! (AMPC)

A fresh prophetic word is being delegated to the Church to articulate Heaven's desire. When a clear directional word has been imparted, it is our place to announce it through an atmosphere of His anointing. This will be part of the bridal calling.

Those anointed with this spirit will begin to speak against sickness, sin, and spiritual corruption. This past season of grooming and refinement has been for this purpose. There has been a sifting of our soul and the establishment of contrition and humility essential to embody extravagant levels of power and authority. The spirit of understanding will bring illumination to this reality and mobilize God's people for this great task.

TWO TRACKS: TRUTH AND LOVE

An issue of great importance consistently emphasized by the Lord is the full manifestation of the Spirit of Truth. As the emerging army of believers, we must learn to embrace truth so the "fog" of deception and delusion would have no place to flourish in the Church.

By girding our loins with the "belt of truth," our foundation in Christ is firmly established. This allows us to then be leaven-free and fully released into His anointing for this seven-year spiritual season. When reports began to circulate out of Lakeland, Florida and it seemed a revival was on the horizon, I asked the Lord about it and received an unusual response. The Spirit impressed upon me the phrase, "It is the last of the old order." Initially I did not fully understand its implication, but greater clarity has developed in recent time.

Based on a prophetic word, our ministry cosponsored a conference with MorningStar Ministries in March 2009 entitled "Honoring the Fathers." The prophetic word came with the promise that a spirit of revival would follow if we esteemed the mothers and fathers of the prior generation. Clearly great spiritual outpourings are forecast for the coming days. We will see more tent meetings, evangelistic crusades, and powerful gatherings in stadiums and churches. However, despite our great appreciation for the healings, miracles, and salvations, what we have seen demonstrated thus far has not modeled nor exhibited the "new thing" that is promised. There is more—much more!

> GREAT SPIRITUAL OUTPOURINGS ARE
> FORECAST FOR THE COMING DAYS.

A PURE PEOPLE

Although the Feast of Pentecost allowed leavened bread, what is coming will maintain an emphasis on the extraction of spiritual leaven. Jesus said:

> *"How is it that you do not understand that I did not speak to you concerning bread? But*

beware of the leaven of the Pharisees and Sadducees." Then they understood that He did not say to beware of the leaven of bread, but of the teaching of the Pharisees and Sadducees (Matthew 16:11-12).

We have seen the realization of Passover, the feast of the first month, and Pentecost, the feast of the third month. Now, we are poised to see the literal fulfillment of the feast of the seventh month—Tabernacles. God will tabernacle in His Bride to do through her all the great and wonderful things He did while on the earth in human form.

> GOD WILL TABERNACLE IN HIS BRIDE TO DO THROUGH HER ALL THE GREAT AND WONDERFUL THINGS HE DID WHILE ON THE EARTH IN HUMAN FORM.

Of the seven churches outlined in Revelation, the Laodicean church most accurately defines this present age. Like Laodicea, our admonition is to be clothed with white garments that the shame of our nakedness would not be revealed; these are representing priestly and divinely powerful apparels by which we clothe ourselves spiritually. To experience Tabernacles is to be "clothed with Christ."

The night is far spent, the day is at hand. Therefore let us cast off the works of darkness, and let us put on the armor of light. Let us walk properly, as in the day, not in revelry and drunkenness, not in lewdness and lust, not in strife and envy. But put on the Lord Jesus Christ, and make no provision for the flesh, to fulfill its lusts (Romans 13:12-14 NKJV).

Our ultimate calling is to be like Him and display His garments of righteousness, sanctification, revelation, and power. This is only achieved through the union experience with God Himself abiding in His Bride. Isaiah prophesied this, saying:

I will rejoice greatly in the Lord, My soul will exult in my God; for He has clothed me with garments of salvation, He has wrapped me with a robe of righteousness, as a bridegroom decks himself with a garland, and as a bride adorns herself with her jewels (Isaiah 61:10).

If we put on holy array, then our motives will carry no misrepresentation or selfish ambition. Either we must learn from history or we will be doomed to repeat it. In times past, many wonderfully anointed leaders stumbled because of the failure to be completely clothed in Christ. We are commissioned at this time to embrace His offering of grace to *"become partakers of the divine nature, having escaped the corruption that is in the world by lust"* (2 Pet. 1:4).

We are to be "galvanized" with Christ! An iron chain is a very powerful tool; however, it can be compromised through corruption and rust. When the iron chain links are galvanized, they are coated with zinc, which is non-corruptible. Galvanized iron then becomes much more powerful because it is no longer subject to corruption; it will endure under the harshest of conditions that would otherwise compromise its integrity.

Likewise, when we *put on the Lord Jesus Christ,* our spirits are *galvanized* with Christ and our flesh is coated with the anointing. Corruption will then take on the incorruptible nature.

> WHEN WE PUT ON THE LORD JESUS CHRIST OUR SPIRITS ARE GALVANIZED WITH CHRIST AND OUR FLESH IS COATED WITH THE ANOINTING.

REMOVING MIXTURE

The Feast of Tabernacles is referenced more often in the Bible than any of the other feasts and is recognized throughout Israel's history as the greatest of her festivals. As I have already pointed out, it is also known as the Feast of the Open Book.

When Moses came to the end of his journey, the Lord commanded him to instruct Israel to open the Book of the Covenant and read it to the new generation since the former generation perished in the wilderness because of unbelief. Only in the Feast of Tabernacles was the book opened and read before the people as a symbolic gesture of the great revelation that will come to the generation that literally fulfills all that this feast represents.

Not only are we called to access the revelations of the "Open Book" but also devour and prophesy them to this final age so that the fullness of the Gentiles may come in. According to Revelation 10:10-11:

> *I took the little book out of the angel's hand and ate it, and in my mouth it was sweet as honey; and when I had eaten it, my stomach was made bitter. And they said to me, "You must prophesy again concerning many peoples and nations and tongues and kings."*

This is none other than the book concealed in Daniel's day and revealed to the end-of-time generation. It is the full stature and revelation of the Lord Jesus Christ. Like the sons of Zadok, the bridal company will minister to the Lord and dine at His table in order to emerge with the discernment necessary to separate the precious from the profane and the clean from the unclean (see Ezek. 44).

From a practical point of view, we should expect tremendous revelatory teachings to surface in the coming days that will take us deep into God's Word and the full revelation of the wonderful things concealed through Daniel but revealed to the Bride. This will present her without spot or wrinkle and cleansed of spiritual leaven.

CHAPTER 8

THE BRIDAL MANDATE

PART OF THE great commission is the harvest of souls through the demonstration of the Spirit's power. Another part is the ministry of deliverance to set captives free and liberate prisoners from spiritual dungeons.

Then there is the ministry of healing, including restoring sight to the blind, unstopping deaf ears, and making lame limbs whole; but it also comprises inner healing of wounds to the soul and the spirit, which can take many forms. These are all wonderful and lofty purposes to which we devote ourselves in preparation and equipping.

But in the process of pursuing the Holy Spirit's power and anointing, we also discover an even higher quest for which we were created—to have intimate relationship and communion with Him. For most people, even some Christians, the Lord Jesus is not a living reality but an inference or an unapproachable influence in a far-distant domain.

He is often spoken or referred to in generalities or coined phrases—such as "the man upstairs"—and remains personally unknown to individuals. Creeds and dogmas are formulated from this form of thinking that convert our walk with the Lord from relationship to religion. We cannot love an ideal or express loyalty to an influence. Most people fail to consciously understand that the Lord is a Person who is perceivably present and ardently desirous of relationship and personal exchange.

> WE CANNOT LOVE AN IDEAL OR
> EXPRESS LOYALTY TO AN INFLUENCE.

While there is a collective acknowledgment of the Lord's existence, there is nevertheless an overriding misperception that He is unknowable or unapproachable on a personal level. That deceiving influence in the Church must be overcome in this generation. It is a form of spiritual wickedness that keeps us from the knowledge of God.

Comprehension of someone is best attained through intimate exchange and shared experiences. A holy dialogue—through spiritually granted access to hear His expressions and experience His Presence—promotes awareness of Him and energizes us from a dead religion to a living relationship.

The Scriptures provide the clear spiritual doctrine that God can be known through personal experience. The pages of the Bible are filled with heroes of the faith who discovered this reality. We find God walking in the Garden with Adam, expressing Himself with Moses through a burning bush, talking with disciples on the road to Emmaus, meeting with His apostle on the way to Damascus, and on the Isle of Patmos. He promised to be with us, even in us until the end of the age. Personal encounters transform and endow us to function in Heaven's supernatural realms, to perpetually walk in God's anointing as well as to sustain that place of relationship and authority.

PERPETUATING THE ANOINTING

Far too often many devoted saints throughout history gave themselves to the work of ministry but somehow lost the intimacy and communion that brought them consistent anointing and power. A loving personality communicating with His people is a dominant theme throughout biblical history. Where He finds a place of receptivity among humans, He shares insight, direction, correction, encouragement, and promises through various manifestations of His Spirit.

> WHERE HE FINDS A PLACE OF RECEPTIVITY AMONG HUMANS, HE SHARES INSIGHT, DIRECTION, CORRECTION, ENCOURAGEMENT, AND PROMISES THROUGH VARIOUS MANIFESTATIONS OF HIS SPIRIT.

Consequently, we must invest ourselves in intimate dialogue and sacred fellowship with the Lord and be completely unwilling to compromise that relationship for any purpose. Notice the apostle Paul's heartfelt desperation. Even after many years of powerful ministry, his passionate desire was to *"know Him and the power of His resurrection and the fellowship of His sufferings"* (Phil. 3:10).

Joined with the Great Commission to bring the Gospel of salvation and power and the more important necessity of having intimate relationship and exchange with the Lord is a third mandate that is perhaps equally important—to be the agency through whom the entire earth is filled with God's glory.

REVELATION OF HIS GLORY

In the days of Moses, the Lord descended upon Mount Sinai in all of His splendor and power in a grand display of His vast greatness. He revealed Himself in this imposing way to impress ancient Israel with His majesty and use them to fill the earth with His glory. Unfortunately, they missed the mark. The Lord was so grieved with their unbelief and disobedience that He was prepared to destroy the entire nation with the exception of Moses.

Because of Moses' intercession, the Lord stayed His hand of judgment but made a profound declaration:

> So the Lord said, "I have pardoned them according to your word; but indeed, as I live, all the earth will be filled with the glory of the Lord" (Numbers 14:20-21).

There must be a generation who cooperates with the Lord to fulfill this solemn oath given so many centuries ago.

It was the Lord's desire to reveal Himself to the entire nation of Israel. The chief longing of His heart is still to present Himself to a holy nation and a royal priesthood and use them to fill the earth with His glory. Thus our directive, along with winning the lost and healing the sick, is to participate with the Holy Spirit in filling the earth with God's glory.

THE YEAR KING UZZIAH DIED

To better understand this great mandate, we can glean key insights from Isaiah 6:

> *In the year of King Uzziah's death I saw the Lord sitting on a throne, lofty and exalted, with the train of His robe filling the temple* (Isaiah 6:1).

The Lord wonderfully blessed King Uzziah until his heart was lifted up in pride. This presumptuous arrogance caused Uzziah to enter the Holy of Holies and attempt to offer incense upon the altar without the priestly anointing and consecration essential for this duty. For this grievous error, God struck Uzziah with leprosy, as observed on his forehead by the priests.

According to Levitical law, when the priests identified leprosy on the forehead of a person, that person was pronounced unclean and required to cover his lips and cry "unclean, unclean" (Lev. 13:43-45).

To comprehend the significance of King Uzziah's transgression, let us begin with the statement of the prophet Isaiah as he stood before the very throne of God witnessing the exchange of the seraphim giving glory to God:

> *And one called out to another and said, "Holy, Holy, Holy, is the Lord of hosts, the whole earth is full of His glory." And the foundations of the thresholds trembled at the voice of him who called out, while the temple was filling with smoke. Then I said, "Woe is me, for I am ruined! Because I am a man of unclean lips, and I live among a people of unclean lips; for my eyes have seen the King, the Lord of hosts"* (Isaiah 6:3-5).

When Isaiah found himself not in the type and shadow on the earth but in the literal Holy of Holies in Heaven, before God's throne, he clearly must have remembered the grotesque and distorted appearance of King Uzziah before his death. With that image in mind, Isaiah in essence stated, "I am like Uzziah, stricken with leprosy; I am likewise unclean and unworthy to stand in this Holy Place."

A DIVINE PROVISION

Interestingly, an angel flew to the very place where Uzziah was stricken, the altar of incense, and extracted coal and applied it to the lips of Isaiah. There was an atoning provision for Isaiah. The Lord had made a redemptive provision allowing atonement and cleansing for the condition in which Isaiah found himself.

There was no correction of the statement made by Isaiah that he was unclean. Rather, the Lord's atoning attribute altered the condition of Isaiah and made him cleansed and worthy to participate in the exchange of glory taking place before the throne of Heaven. Uzziah entered the Holy Place on earth with pride and presumption, while Isaiah appeared with lowliness and contrition.

FILLING THE TEMPLE WITH GLORY

Then the Lord asked Isaiah the question:

> *"Whom shall I send, and who will go for Us?"*
> *Then I said, "Here am I. Send me!"* (Isaiah 6:8)

When Isaiah yielded himself to this commission, he heard the unusual instruction coming from the Lord concerning the eyes and ears of the people of his generation. They were to be rendered spiritually blind and deaf. Grace was not given for that generation to see with their eyes nor hear with their ears God's unfolding plan of redemption and His determination to fellowship with a body of people on the earth, spreading Kingdom authority.

Jesus emphatically quoted this passage in His discourse to the religious leaders during His earthly ministry as well. He said:

> For this reason they could not believe, for Isaiah said again, "He has blinded their eyes and He hardened their heart, so that they would not see with their eyes and perceive with their heart, and be converted and I heal them." These things Isaiah said because he saw His glory, and he spoke of Him (John 12:39-41).

From among all the people living in Jesus' day, only a small remnant received the Messiah and the life He imparted (see Matt. 13:14-15; Mark 4:12; Luke 8:10).

As Isaiah's instruction continues, the Lord states "lest they see with their eyes, and hear with their ears, and understand with their heart, and return and be healed" (Isa. 6:10 NKJV). Healing occurs when our eyes and ears are opened and our hearts are permitted to understand.

HEALING THE BREACH

Healing is not merely the mending of broken bodies and emotions, but more importantly the restoration of the breach between God and humanity. That is why our adversary has so emphatically opposed the impartation of revelatory gifts.

We can only participate in this Kingdom plan to the extent that we "see" and "hear" with spirit "eyes and ears," thereby eliciting comprehension to our hearts. This insight cannot be the mechanical repetition of words with merely an intellectual perception of the Almighty's sovereignty and glory. We are recruited when we as "overcoming" saints are anointed with the spirit of wisdom and revelation. Then we comprehend and experience the unveiling of God's kingly authority, His heavenly dominion, and His great glory and give expression to it.

> ## WE ARE RECRUITED WHEN WE AS "OVERCOMING" SAINTS ARE ANOINTED WITH THE SPIRIT OF WISDOM AND REVELATION.

The prophet Isaiah was granted the personal privilege of seeing Heaven's design at the throne of God as seraphim declared to one another: *"Holy, Holy, Holy is the Lord of Hosts."* They were allowed to see with their eyes demonstrations of His majesty and authority and give expression to it. Their words began to fill the temple with smoke and glory through the witness of their eyes and the utterance of their lips conveying the revelation of God sitting upon His throne in absolute and perfect supremacy and sovereignty.

As the seraphim gave glory to God and God received the glory due Him, more of His divine attributes emanated to them, causing an even greater demonstration of praise and glory. This Kingdom exchange and heavenly design continued filling the atmosphere with the glory and illumination of God until the entire temple was saturated with the appearance and revelation of His glory.

That is the fashion of Heaven to be transferred to earth and our assignment—to create an atmosphere on the earth that is consistent with His nature and character in which He can dwell. If we can fulfill this mandate, all the other purposes and desires for which we long will naturally be established and achieved by His Presence and anointing resting in us.

> OUR ASSIGNMENT—TO CREATE AN ATMOSPHERE ON THE EARTH THAT IS CONSISTENT WITH HIS NATURE AND CHARACTER IN WHICH HE CAN DWELL.

Certainly, Isaiah must have been compelled to likewise participate in this exchange of glory, yet he recognized the unworthiness and impurity of his own lips to give glory to God in such a holy surrounding. Fortunately, the provision of Heaven purified him and removed his uncleanness, allowing him to give glory to God. We have been cleansed by the blood of Jesus Christ and presented before Him "holy and blameless and beyond reproach."

WHO WILL GO FOR US?

This commissioning of Isaiah was not as a prophet. The Scriptures plainly report that he was already functioning in the office of a prophet long before the experience of Isaiah 6. Perhaps, Isaiah was being asked, "Who will go for Us?" to begin filling the earth with the glory of the Lord of hosts as witnessed in Heaven before God's throne—on Earth as it is in Heaven.

Isaiah observed the atmosphere surrounding Heaven's throne. He saw Heaven's design created around the kingship and dominion of the Lord and the unveiling of His glory as seen by those witnessing the nature and character of His kingly authority.

In a similar way, this same atmosphere must be created on earth in His Bride. We experientially comprehend the Lord's holy attributes then give expression to what we have seen and heard. Then our words possess life and spirit to fill the earth with His glory. That is the will of Heaven being done on earth. It is the creation of the environment in which the Lord is able to dwell. This eternal atmosphere of glory and beauty provides a surrounding consistent with His divine nature and holy character. This is our lofty mandate.

CHAPTER 9

EXPERIENTIAL TRUTH

THROUGHOUT THE WORLD, millions recognize this present day as the consummation of the ages and God's grand finale with latter rain truth. The Scriptures tell us that the Spirit of Truth is promised as our heritage to guide us into all truth and to show us things to come.

> *But when He, the Spirit of Truth, comes, He will guide you into all the truth; for He will not speak on His own initiative, but whatever He hears, He will speak; and He will disclose to you what is to come. He will glorify Me, for He will take of Mine and will disclose it to you. All things that the Father has are Mine; therefore I said that He takes of Mine and will disclose it to you* (John 16:13-15).

The deep things of God are known only to Him, but are revealed to us through His Spirit. That is the promise of First Corinthians 2. Therefore, it is our expectation to witness an unprecedented outpouring of His Spirit that unfolds last-day mysteries that will perfect the Bride and empower the sons of the Kingdom.

Mere human knowledge is not sufficient to bring in the great harvest. We must be endowed with God's supernatural provision that is clearly promised for this hour. To do so, every saint of God must come to the realization that Christ is "all in all."

> EVERY SAINT OF GOD MUST COME TO THE REALIZATION THAT CHRIST IS "ALL IN ALL."

He is Light; He is the Way, Truth, Life; He is the Resurrection; He is Wisdom; He is Righteousness; He is Goodness; He is Understanding; He is Alpha and Omega; He is the Beginning and the End; He is All in All.

To merely acknowledge these as doctrinal truth is not sufficient. They must become experiential reality through personal encounters with the living Christ. The Lord is standing at the door knocking with a personal invitation for profound fellowship and the unveiling of latter rain revelation. For those who will forsake all else to dine with Him, this will be an age of greater glory and personal transformation into His very image.

SOARING WITH HIM

Indisputably, our great desire is to soar in the Spirit and obtain revelations of God's nature, power, strategy, and insight. However, to best accommodate this great privilege, we must be firmly "rooted and grounded" in Him. According to the Holy Spirit's admonition spoken to me while in Canada, "Go deep in order to go high!"

We *must* be:

1. Rooted and grounded in love (see Eph. 3:17).

2. Rooted and grounded in faith (see Col. 1:23).

3. Rooted and grounded in truth (see 2 Tim. 3:15).

I cannot overemphasize the importance of these three foundations in order for us to be trusted with the Lord's secrets. We are living in a generation privileged to be endowed with the spirit of revelation leading us into comprehension of Kingdom mysteries. To facilitate this, we must be established in truth, faith, and love to properly understand and appropriate His heart.

The more firmly we are grounded, the more capable we become to penetrate Heaven by the spirit of wisdom and revelation and embrace insight with understanding. The pursuit of truth will lead us to places in the Spirit yielding the fruit of righteousness and power. The quest for knowledge without truth can result in pride and arrogance.

A clear distinction between the two is essential for personal transformation and maturity. When we cultivate a love for truth, we will not be turned over to deluding influences that will characterize those who have rejected Christ in the last days (see 2 Thess. 2:10-11).

IN THE SPIRIT

Presently, many believers are oppressed with feelings of hopelessness, fear, doubt, and other bondages exploited by the enemy. It is the Holy Spirit's desire to carry us above this realm, into the Spirit, where our blessings and provisions are discovered in Christ. In this higher realm, we embrace hope to displace hopelessness and fear is overcome by faith.

> OUR BLESSINGS AND PROVISIONS
> ARE DISCOVERED IN CHRIST.

This truth is evidenced in both the Old and New Testaments. On one occasion, the prophet Elisha boldly encountered the king of Aram and his armies. He did so without timidity or reservation. Conversely, his servant was battling issues of fear and doubt. That is, until he was carried above that realm to discover the more accurate spiritual perspective. God's governmental leader helped his servant above the soulish realm of anxiety and uncertainty by saying:

> *"Do not fear, for those who are with us are more than those who are with them." Then Elisha prayed and said, "O Lord, I pray, open his eyes that he may see." And the Lord opened the servant's eyes and he saw; and behold, the mountain was full of horses and chariots of fire all around Elisha* (2 Kings 6:16-17).

When the prophet prayed for his servant, the Spirit's impartation allowed the servant access to the realm of faith and supernatural vision. As a result, he was changed and his perspective radically transformed. The limited view this servant previously held is the only one his adversary, the devil, wanted him to comprehend.

Likewise, the enemy desires that we see only the seemingly insurmountable obstacles and difficulties that stand between our destiny and us. Therefore, when we walk by the Spirit, we will not carry out the deeds of our fallen nature.

In Elisha's servant, the above experience radically affected his life—his eyes were opened and he "saw." In a similar way, the Holy Spirit desires that we carry this anointing that opens eyes and distinguishes between the deceptions of our adversary and the provision of our Redeemer.

Experientially comprehending our Source unleashes supernatural faith to live above this worldly realm and access the heavenly dimension.

> EXPERIENTIALLY COMPREHENDING OUR SOURCE UNLEASHES SUPERNATURAL FAITH TO LIVE ABOVE THIS WORLDLY REALM AND ACCESS THE HEAVENLY DIMENSION.

MARIA WOODWORTH-ETTER

The Holy Spirit has made it profoundly clear to me that this powerful woman's ministry was a prototype or forerunner introduction to the mature sons and daughters of God. Visions and revelations seemed to be an integral part of Maria Woodworth-Etter's ministry. Both those who were saved and others who attended the meetings to ridicule and mock her ministry experienced this realm of the Holy Spirit. It is well documented that many saints who were bound by various forms of oppression and sickness were delivered through their supernatural encounter with the heavenly realm.

When this dimension was opened in her meetings, a reverential awe permeated the auditorium and forever changed each one touched. Many individuals who discovered that "open door" made lifelong commitments to the Lord. It is reported that some actually received the gift of speaking other languages and were commissioned as missionaries to the nations.

Woodworth-Etter reported that prophetic utterances were given to young and old alike concerning future events, many of which took place within days or weeks. Others returned with supernatural knowledge and insight they had no way of knowing within themselves.

In each case, people were captured by the humility and contrition demonstrated in the lives of those who encountered God in this deeper spiritual arena. No one boasted or acted superficially; only reverence, contrition, and a life of consecration to God was evidenced. Even so, great joy also characterized this remarkable woman's life and ministry.

In one particular meeting held in St. Louis, Missouri, the people of the city were particularly harsh in their treatment of this precious sister and her ministry team. The meetings were attended by some of the most hardened characters in the city. In her journal, Maria Woodworth-Etter wrote: "Men stood on the seats with hats on, cigars and pipes in their mouths, coats off and sleeves rolled up...women wore dirty aprons...and bare armed...they would shoot off firecrackers and when we sang, they sang even louder and when we prayed, they clapped their hands and cheered. They carry pistols and clubs and were ready to kill us and tear down the tent."

However, the end of her story is quite different. The Lord faithfully heard the prayers of His devoted saints and responded by opening the heavens and giving people visions of Heaven and hell. Through the Holy Spirit, the people encountered a spiritual dimension.

The results were stunning, according to Woodworth-Etter: "The fear of God came upon the multitude. The sweat came on their faces and they stood as though in a trance; men began to take their pipes out of their mouths and their hats off. The women began to cover their bare necks and arms with aprons. They felt they stood naked and guilty before God. They began to get off the seats (from standing) and sit down but some fell and lay like dead."

Evidence of a tangible touch from the third heaven was apparent and easily discerned. This was true both for those who were saved and those who were not. The fruit was visible through the people's responses and by its consistency with the Scriptures. Often it is recorded in Maria Woodworth-Etter's writings that sinners and saints alike would cry out in reverential fear when the heavenly dimension was opened to them.

OUR HOPE

A phenomenal opportunity to encounter and embrace our heavenly Father is being given to the Church around the world today. It is one that must be welcomed and protected. With the dawning of this new day in church history, the anointing of Heaven is disbursed in the spiritual atmosphere so those truly seeking truth can lay hold of it and obtain great insight with understanding. As sons of the Kingdom ask with sincerity for this deposit, it will be received. Our spiritual eyes will be illumined to see the Scriptures from Heaven's perspective, not merely man's.

> A PHENOMENAL OPPORTUNITY TO ENCOUNTER AND EMBRACE OUR HEAVENLY FATHER IS BEING GIVEN TO THE CHURCH AROUND THE WORLD TODAY.

The spiritual realities that are being birthed in the earth now will have no end. They will literally flow into the millennial age and the coming manifestation of His Kingdom on the earth.

Though we do not know when those days will be fully revealed, we do know that the purposes now being birthed will advance directly into that age. We will begin to taste the good Word of God and the power of the age to come. Like the beloved disciple John in his notable revelations, we will be allowed to eat the Open Book containing the full manifestation of the Lord's redemptive plans and purposes. This will be the tasting of His Kingdom Word and a demonstration of Kingdom might in order to wonderfully introduce the Lord Jesus in truth and power to an entire generation.

> "SONSHIP" IS MUCH MORE THAN
> A MESSAGE; IT IS A RELATIONSHIP.

It is my heart's desire and ambition to encourage every believer to pursue this God-given reality. "Sonship" is much more than a message; it is a relationship—the relationship of a son to his Father—and the way to sonship is not by "doing" but by "becoming."

CHAPTER 10

THE LATTER GLORY

SOMETIMES THE GREATEST prophecies come in the midst of the most unlikely circumstances. Following Israel's Babylonian captivity, the remnant who saw the majesty and splendor of Solomon's temple likely found it difficult to believe Haggai's prophecy when he said:

> *Speak now to Zerubbabel the son of Shealtiel, governor of Judah, and to Joshua the son of Jehozadak, the high priest, and to the remnant of the people saying, "Who is left among you who saw this temple in its former glory? And how do you see it now? Does it not seem to you like nothing in comparison? But now take courage, Zerubbabel," declares the Lord, "take courage also, Joshua son of Jehozadak, the high priest, and all you people of the land take courage," declares the Lord, "and work; for I am with you," declares the Lord of hosts.*

"As for the promise which I made you when you came out of Egypt, My Spirit is abiding in your midst; do not fear!" For thus says the Lord of hosts, "Once more in a little while, I am going to shake the heavens and the earth, the sea also and the dry land. I will shake all the nations; and they will come with the wealth of all nations, and I will fill this house with glory," says the Lord of hosts. "The silver is Mine and the gold is Mine," declares the Lord of hosts. "The latter glory of this house will be greater than the former," says the Lord of hosts, "and in this place I will give peace," declares the Lord of hosts (Haggai 2:2-9).

Nothing before or since has ever compared to the wonder of Solomon's temple. Even so, this incredible prophecy points to a time of extraordinary restoration and promise. The glory of the restored temple was to be greater than the former. What made it greater? Our Messiah Himself came to the restored temple and taught of His Father's Kingdom and displayed a visible representation of the invisible God. That is the greater glory!

Today many still find it difficult to believe that the glory of this present latter-day house will exceed the glory of the early apostolic Church. Nevertheless, God has promised it and His Spirit will see it fulfilled.

God *will* Tabernacle in a body of people in these last days to exhibit His holy character and do exploits that will exceed any previously demonstrated in human history. We must begin to gear up for this reality.

THE PLUMB LINE OF TRUTH

Through the prophecies of Haggai and Zechariah, a small band of people were determined to fulfill God's Word. One of those great promises is found in Zechariah 4, stating:

> *For who has despised the day of small things? But these seven will be glad when they see the plumb line in the hand of Zerubbabel—these are the eyes of the Lord which range to and fro throughout the earth* (Zechariah 4:10).

The plumb line of truth is now in the hands of our "Zerubbabel." This great leader is a spiritual type of Christ. The "hands of Zerubbabel" laid the foundation of the Church and now the same "hands" will bring the capstone with shouts of "grace, grace."

This points to the anointing, power, and authority demonstrated by the Lord Jesus Himself to establish the Church's foundation being once again demonstrated at the end of the age to bring the capstone or closing out of church history and the introduction of the Kingdom realm. How can this be achieved? Only through amazing and exceptional favor with shouts of grace, grace!

As I have already emphasized, the Feast of Tabernacles is a spiritual prototype of this reality illustrating God's manifest presence. It will function through a sold-out radical people called the Bride of Christ. This season will see tremendous demonstrations of the Spirit of Truth as the leaven of tradition and man-made teaching is extracted.

> THIS SEASON WILL SEE TREMENDOUS DEMONSTRATIONS OF THE SPIRIT OF TRUTH AS THE LEAVEN OF TRADITION AND MAN-MADE TEACHING IS EXTRACTED.

There is an angelic host working closely with the Spirit of Truth to establish revelatory truth in the hearts of believers and in the nations of the earth. Our resolution must be to continually follow the Word that perpetually proceeds from the Father's heart.

THE WORD OF SEPARATION

The Living Word described in Hebrews 4:12 is a discerner of the thoughts and intents of the heart. This is an expression of God's manifest presence. It is not a place in which we give lip service that is not consistent with the desires of our hearts. We saw a token portrayal of this reality in the last generation when anointed vessels stood before God's people and revealed secrets of the heart known only to them and God. This was not merely a nice spiritual gift but a token of the end-time scenario when the Living Word takes up residence in a body of people to do the greater works.

Our council is to cooperate with Heaven and do only what we see the Father doing and say only what we hear

Him saying. The Lord is opening our eyes and ears with the spirit of understanding so that our discernment is taken to greater levels to accomplish this purpose.

There will be righteous leaders emerging today who will be shepherds of love and truth. It will not be their intent to harm or abuse the sheep. Many of these leaders will have known failure and profound restoration through which they discovered divine love. They will have been healed of their brokenness, but in the process, contrition will have become their standard.

The righteous shepherds will lead the sheep to calm waters so that the Body of Christ can discover God in personal ways. Many of the shepherds will be emerging from obscure and isolated places. They will bring an anointing to calm troubled waters presently in the Church and will carry authority to speak into people's hearts.

> THE HARVEST OF SOULS AND THE
> HARVEST OF PROMISES BEGIN WITH
> THE HUMBLE AND CONTRITE AND
> THOSE WHO TREMBLE AT HIS WORD.

The preparation process has been long and difficult, but God has given us new life at different times to encourage us to continue to press into Him. Now the Lord of the Harvest has risen. Everyone is called to have a role in the harvest; the harvest of souls and the harvest of promises begin with the humble and contrite and those who tremble at His Word (see Isa. 66:1-2).

STANDING IN THE GAP
FOR THIS GENERATION

The eyes of the Lord are roving to and fro looking for a righteous agency on the earth to stand in the gap. The Lord is asking, "Is there no man when I call? Is there anyone to answer? I am speaking; is there anyone listening? Is My hand shortened at all that it cannot redeem? Or have I no power to deliver? Don't you know who I am?"

There will be a remnant of people on the earth who hear and respond to this call. According to Isaiah 50:2, the Lord asked:

> *Why was there no man when I came? When I called, why was there none to answer? Is My hand so short that it cannot ransom? Or have I no power to deliver? Behold, I dry up the sea with My rebuke, I make the rivers a wilderness; their fish stink for lack of water and die of thirst.*

God's Spirit can change things quickly. He is giving His people an instructed tongue that we may sustain the weary with a word from Him. He is presently awakening many disciples (instructed ones) morning by morning to give them eyes to see and ears to hear (see Isa. 50:4).

The righteous prayer of Job intervened for those around him despite their folly.

It is time the fortune of God's people be restored as well. The Lord turned the captivity of Job and restored double when he prayed for his friends. We are entering the season of the double portion.

> *For I will accept him so that I may not do with you according to your folly, because you have not spoken of Me what is right, as My servant Job has. ...The Lord restored the fortunes of Job when he prayed for his friends, and the Lord increased all that Job had twofold* (Job 42:8,10).

Many in the Church are coming to the end of a time of pruning and judgment as it is beginning in the world. God's desire is for our light to shine brightly as many people head our way in this dark season. It is time for those who overcome to arise with a measure of His glory resting upon them. This will literally be the fulfillment of Daniel's prophecy when he wrote:

> *Those who have insight will shine brightly like the brightness of the expanse of heaven, and those who lead the many to righteousness, like the stars forever and ever* (Daniel 12:3).

It is time for the accomplishment of divine purposes and a wave of harvest. The Lord is laying claim to this generation of young people as well as the seasoned and mature. It will be both the Joshuas and the Calebs. The Lord is healing the fracture He has created in a third-day harvest of the wounded and persecuted. His will is being accomplished in a mighty way so that a harvest can be achieved.

Trials in the earth will increase while at the same time end-time truths from the Book of Revelation become increasingly clear. Great understanding will be delegated to the Church concerning these mysteries. Revelation is a love letter to the Lord's Bride and prepares her to be joined to Him.

DESTINED FOR VICTORY

The Lord has already triumphed over the adversary and made a public spectacle of him. Many in a firstfruits harvest will comprehend that reality more fully and appropriate it. The Lord delegates His victory to us when we are joined to Him.

> THE LORD HAS ALREADY TRIUMPHED
> OVER THE ADVERSARY AND MADE
> A PUBLIC SPECTACLE OF HIM.

One of our greatest opportunities is to no longer be considered the Lord's servants but His friends. We have a Friend who is eternally postured on His throne of victory and authority. We desperately need a more complete vision of this reality to fully activate our faith. Commissioning from the Throne Room can be a living reality as promised through God's Word. He is saying, "Come up here!"

The Lord's Church is required to discern the times and seasons by possessing the mind of Christ for this day. It isn't His desire to conceal His plans and purposes. Instead, He is revealing great understanding so even the worldly may see God's blessing and wisdom resting on His people. That is what the grooming of the last decade has been intended to accomplish. The pain of our past is the preparation for our future.

Brokenness without the spirit of understanding breeds hopelessness, but brokenness with understanding imparts the hope of our calling in God. The Lord's Spirit has been pruning and uprooting our fallen nature and carnal plans in order to inject His own pure nature. His ultimate purpose is to reveal the Fatherhood of God and make us His mature sons and daughters.

Though it seems God's remnant have failed in many ways, these years have actually cultivated humility. The arm of the flesh and our own strength cannot accomplish the end-time mandate. It will not be by the might of man nor the power of our own ingenuity, but by His Spirit alone. Our job is to yield and learn to cooperate with Him.

> *"A Redeemer will come to Zion, and to those who turn from transgression in Jacob," declares the Lord. "As for Me, this is My covenant with them," says the Lord: "My Spirit which is upon you, and My words which I have put in your mouth shall not depart from your mouth, nor from the mouth of your offspring, nor from the mouth of your offspring's offspring," says the Lord, "from now and forever"* (Isaiah 59:20-21).

Like Jacob, the Lord has destroyed our dependence upon human strength and changed our nature. A new name is being given, according to Revelation 2:17, to those who overcome in this fashion. Then we enjoy a perpetual covenant of His Presence. With His words in our mouth we become His voice on earth.

CHAPTER 11

GOING BEHIND THE VEIL

A FEW YEARS ago, the Lord gave me a wonderful experience that I believe depicts the present calling of many within the Church. The radical remnant is being prepared to go behind the veil to understand great and mighty things which we currently do not know. These will experience Jeremiah 33:3 and receive key strategies and insights directly from the Lord that are of paramount importance. This prophetic Scripture declares:

> *Call to Me and I will answer you and show you great and mighty things, fenced in and hidden, which you do not know (do not distinguish and recognize, have knowledge of and understand) (AMPC).*

In the visionary experience, I saw the Lord walking in a determined manner, but I could only see Him from the back. He was wearing a dark blue robe that reached to the ground. The color seemed to indicate His deep revelatory nature. Because I was walking from behind, I was unable to see His face. I suppose that could be good in that He was leading and I was following.

As I approached Him I knew exactly who He was. Other people were seemingly around, but I paid little attention to them. As I approached Him I threw my arms around Him and placed my head on his right shoulder with a great sense of affection and friendship. It would have been nice to simply remain there for a few years. It is important to remember this is an experience to help illustrate the relationship and affections this company will have with the Lord.

He allowed the loving embrace for a few moments, then pointed to a wall directly in front of us. It had a stone or tile-like appearance. I noticed at the base of the wall an area that seemed to have been opened once before but was now sealed and "hidden" with small stones, flat rocks, and scraps of paper. It was as though the wall was there the entire time, but it took the Lord pointing it out to highlight my attention. I began to remove the paper, stones, and flat rocks and discovered that it was an access to a chamber behind the wall.

As I continued to dig, the tile and stone material could be easily removed. Once the hole was large enough for me to pass through, I discovered a room filled with thousands of ancient scrolls, parchments, journals, and books.

I inherently knew this library of priceless materials had been primarily preserved for our day and contained key secrets in walking closely and intimately with the Lord. It will be a fulfillment of Isaiah 48:6-7 saying:

> *You have heard; look at all this. And you, will you not declare it? I proclaim to you new things from this time, even hidden things which you have not known. They are created now and not long ago; and before today you have not heard them, so that you will not say, "Behold, I knew them."*

Great forerunners like the patriarch Enoch were allowed to go behind the veil and read the writings of Heaven contained in these books. Not only do they portray an intimate walk with the Lord, but also hidden secrets involving creation, time, space, matter, and tremendous insights into the Scripture that we must contend for and give ourselves wholeheartedly to apprehend.

THREE KEY SCRIPTURES

In the center of the room was a wooden stake about six feet in height and a parchment made from what seemed like a small piece of leather attached to it. I knew something important was written on the parchment. I could read three Scriptures that were inscribed. They were Jude, Psalm 68, and First Kings 3.

Each of these passages could have a variety of meanings on multiple levels inherent with each individual. However, I believe there is a clear warning being issued that highlights the characteristics of both true and false forms of leadership that can be identified through the Book of Jude. There are three counterfeit spirits pinpointed in this vital book that we must understand and identify. The spirits of Cain, Balaam, and Korah are distinguished as New Testament adversaries having the following characteristics:

- Cain—sincere form of religious activity with an absence of spiritual revelation as to what God truly desires.

- Balaam—attempting to curse what God has blessed and utilizing spiritual gifts for personal gain.

- Korah—a rebellious form of self-promotion.

> THE LORD'S SPIRIT HAS ISSUED CLEAR WARNINGS ABOUT SOLELY RELYING UPON HUMAN INGENUITY AND GIFTING AS A SUBSTITUTE FOR THE TRUE AND LEGITIMATE APOSTOLIC MINISTRY.

The Lord's Spirit has issued clear warnings about solely relying upon human ingenuity and gifting as a substitute for the true and legitimate apostolic ministry illustrated in the Book of Acts. Very often a false spirit will preempt the release of the genuine with some very convincing qualities and attempt to sway many to its following. We are admonished in Scripture to judge fruit and the signs of the true apostolic ministry based in humility and a Christlike nature.

Authentic apostolic ministry will promote the revelation of Jesus Christ and build His Kingdom with the undiluted Gospel of the Kingdom confirmed with miracles, signs, and wonders. The early apostles were vindicated by the Holy Spirit:

> *And now, Lord, take note of their threats, and grant that Your bond-servants may speak Your word with all confidence, while You extend Your hand to heal, and signs and wonders take place through the name of Your holy servant Jesus* (Acts 4:29-30).

SUPERNATURAL WISDOM AND INSIGHT: A HEARING HEART

I believe there are many who will be commissioned in a manner similar to the way Solomon was set apart and endowed with significant spiritual insight and understanding. Solomon's wise prayer was a more than just natural human wisdom and intelligence. Careful examination reveals that he asked God for the ability to perpetually hear the Spirit's voice. He prayed:

> *So give Your servant an understanding mind and a hearing heart to judge Your people, that I may discern between good and bad. For who is able to judge and rule this Your great people?* (1 Kings 3:9 AMPC)

The Scripture expresses that he received a "hearing heart" allowing him to walk with wisdom and supernatural comprehension during his days of leadership. We desperately need a similar impartation.

A PSALM FOR THE BRIDE

There are numerous significant truths illustrated in Psalm 68. Primarily it is pointing to God's justice beginning to be exemplified in the earth rendering blessings for those walking in righteousness and judgment on those walking in unrighteousness. It also prophetically highlights the glorious consummation of the ages with the promised "latter rain" outpouring to fully appropriate God's inheritance. It speaks of people coming out of slavery and bondage to be set free with the purity and freedom of the "dove company."

> *The earth quaked; the heavens also dropped rain at the presence of God; Sinai itself quaked at the presence of God, the God of Israel. You shed abroad a plentiful rain, O God; You confirmed Your inheritance when it was parched. Your creatures settled in it; You provided in Your goodness for the poor, O God. ...When you lie down among the sheepfolds, you are like the wings of a dove covered with silver, and its pinions with glistening gold* (Psalm 68:8-10,13).

It also points to the "spirit of the fathers" being released and restoring us to a place of intimacy and fellowship previously known by our apostolic fathers. That is the function of the spirit and power of Elijah as prophesied in Malachi 4.

> TRUE AND GENUINE SPIRITUAL FATHERS
> ARE SOON TO EMERGE WITH A HEART
> OF COMPASSION AND HUMILITY THAT
> PREPARES A GENERATION FOR INTIMATE
> RELATIONSHIP WITH THE LORD.

We have been largely known as a "fatherless" generation. However, true and genuine spiritual fathers are soon to emerge with a heart of compassion and humility that prepares a generation for intimate relationship with the Lord. These fathers will have the ability to impart spiritual gifts and awaken the seeds of desire and hunger for the Lord and the things of His Spirit. A teacher provides information, but a father imparts a blessing.

CHAPTER 12

FLOURISHING DURING DAYS OF DARKNESS

THIS IS PERHAPS the most important generation in human history, comparable in importance with the day of the Lord's death and resurrection—the generation that will witness the return of Christ and fulfill all that was promised for that age. These are both sobering and exciting times requiring our full attention and sincere responses.

VESSELS OF HONOR

But in a great house there are not only vessels of gold and silver, but also of wood and clay, some for honor and some for dishonor. Therefore if anyone cleanses himself from the latter, he will be a vessel for honor, sanctified and useful for the Master, prepared for every good work (2 Timothy 2:20-21 NKJV).

The end-time scenario is taking shape and the players are starting to take their position in the dramatic unfolding of events prophetically observed by prophets throughout history. Hunger and desire to become vessels of honor is being imparted to those given the opportunity to participate. It is our prayer that each person will respond with favor and give the Holy Spirit permission to fully clothe them with Himself. This will make us the instruments of His warfare and useful to the Master for every good work.

> HUNGER AND DESIRE TO BECOME VESSELS OF HONOR IS BEING IMPARTED TO THOSE GIVEN THE OPPORTUNITY TO PARTICIPATE.

The Scripture clearly outlines, directly and through types and shadows, the consecration and sanctification necessary to become vessels in whom the Lord will find His rest and through whom He will do His greater works. From among the various redemptive names illustrated in the Old Testament, Jehovah Shammah, The Lord Who is Present, is the one with highlighted emphasis for this hour. When the promise of this redemptive name is realized, the Lord is fully present, bringing with Him all of the other redemptive attributes inherent in His nature.

The Lord is our Provider, Healer, Banner, Sanctifier, Peace, Shepherd, Righteousness, Recompense, Defense as the Lord who smites, and the Lord of Hosts orchestrating the armies of God providing a canopy of protection around those who are His sons and daughters. All of His attributes will be on display in amplified form during our watch.

AN OPEN-DOOR INVITATION

There is a flourishing sense of anticipation and purpose concerning the days in which we are living. The marked increase in the intensity and focus within many Christians relates to the birthing of Kingdom purposes in our nation and throughout the earth. Some individuals are experiencing measures of increase in anointing and various expressions of outpouring to quicken and prepare us for the next wave of the Spirit.

I was recently allowed by the Spirit to witness individuals being taken "behind the veil" and shown great and mighty things reserved for the end time.

> *After these things I looked, and behold, a door standing open in heaven, and the first voice which I had heard, like the sound of a trumpet speaking with me, said, "Come up here, and I will show you what must take place after these things"* (Revelation 4:1).

The objective and commission given to these individuals is to spiritually understand the mysteries associated with these great truths and convey them to the Body of Christ. That is the hopeful aspiration of this book—to awaken God's people to their destiny and create desire to be groomed for their purpose.

We prophetically decree that it is now time to begin to fulfill Revelation 4:1 and Jeremiah 33:3. As many saints call upon Him, He will show great and awesome things which we presently do not know. The truths associated with this reality are quite significant and provide keys that unlock prominent mysteries of Heaven's Kingdom. Many individuals being allowed this experience have gone through the preparation and refining described in this book and essential for this weighty responsibility.

It is difficult to adequately express the importance of being clothed with the garment of humility in the execution of this commission and the sharing of great mysteries imparted in this hour.

HIS BANNER OF LOVE

As the experience continued, the Holy Spirit revealed how the sharing of Kingdom truths with the Body of Christ was likened to the preparation of a great banqueting table being set for the Lord and His Bride. Seemingly, the "implements and banners" that were being revealed to this group somehow were utilized in the adornment of the banqueting table, particularly around the area that was clearly recognized as the "seat of honor." Naturally, these things are shown in symbolic form to illustrate truth that will help us in the hour and the responsibility being delegated to us by the Holy Spirit.

One of the banners highlighted depicted a picture of the High Priest in all of his adornment with the breast plate, golden miter, and other garments. When the banner was displayed, a voice spoke with clarity and determined purpose and stated, "My banner over you is Love."

> *Like an apple tree among the trees of the forest,*
> *so is my beloved among the young men. In his*
> *shade I took great delight and sat down, and*
> *his fruit was sweet to my taste. He has brought*
> *me to his banquet hall, and his banner over me*
> *is love* (Song of Solomon 2:3-4).

There will be many allowed to go behind the veil, to obtain and experience expressions of His divine love that will transcend anything that we presently know. It will be a greater comprehension of His love and heavenly design. A literal fulfillment of John 17:26—*that we may love Him with the love wherewith the Father did love Him.* His love for us will supply the essential spiritual provisions necessary to see us through to our promises.

THERE WILL BE MANY ALLOWED
TO GO BEHIND THE VEIL.

This central truth is an emphasis of the Holy Spirit pointing us to a form of genuine unity with Him that will also birth brotherly love and fraternal affection. Jealousy and selfish ambition have no place in the joining of individuals and ministries for the purpose of pursuing a higher mandate and greater fruitfulness during the end-time generation. Throughout the Church there is an aligning of people and ministries that will produce a much higher anointing and authority in the realm of the Spirit.

LIGHT IN DARKNESS

One needs to only look at the evening news to discern the hour in which we are living , which clearly points to the many biblical prophecies foretelling and describing a day of profound significance. Just as the Bible describes, all things are being shaken so that those things which remain can stand under the scrutiny and pressure of the harvest generation.

The prophet Zechariah foretells a unique day known only to the Lord that is neither day nor night—a day in which light and darkness become apparent at the same time. It is a significant day in which individuals will become the light of the world displaying the bright and virtuous attributes of God Himself.

> *In that day there will be no light; the luminaries will dwindle. For it will be a unique day which is known to the Lord, neither day nor night, but it will come about that at evening time there will be light* (Zechariah 14:6-7).

This day is so remarkable that only the Holy Spirit can make ready a company of people to meet the challenges and spiritual demands of this hour. As it is written, "at evening time it shall be light." This is the "evening time" of human history and the light of God is about to shine.

> THIS IS THE "EVENING TIME" OF
> HUMAN HISTORY AND THE LIGHT
> OF GOD IS ABOUT TO SHINE.

Many of the events that have taken place throughout history have provided a rehearsal for the confrontation between light and darkness as the Holy Spirit orchestrates the training of His army. Likewise, our adversary is also providing polluted authority to those who have set themselves in opposition to the Lord Jesus and His end-time mandates.

A THREEFOLD MANDATE

As I have shared thus far, there are many purposes for which we are being equipped and prepared. However, three most notable divine mandates begin to emerge with emphasis. As noted, our highest purpose and the one instrumental in allowing us to achieve all other purposes is to know God as personally and intimately as He may be known. There is an open door and a call to come up higher to a place of fellowship and exchange with the Creator and establish friendship with God.

> THERE IS AN OPEN DOOR AND A CALL TO
> COME UP HIGHER TO A PLACE OF FELLOWSHIP
> AND EXCHANGE WITH THE CREATOR
> AND ESTABLISH FRIENDSHIP WITH GOD.

From that place of communion, we receive the unveiling of His nature and attributes as not merely intellectual perceptions but the revelation and comprehension of His Person. It was Isaiah's great privilege to see Heaven's design before the throne of God; there, Seraphim spoke one to another declaring, "Holy, Holy, Holy is the Lord of Hosts."

They were allowed to see with their eyes the demonstrations of His majesty and authority and give expression to it. Their words began to fill the temple with smoke and glory by witnessing with their eyes and expressing with their lips the revelation of God sitting upon His throne in absolute and perfect supremacy and sovereignty.

As the seraphim gave glory to Him and He received the glory due Him, more of his divine attributes began to be revealed causing an even greater expression of praise and glory. This Kingdom exchange and heavenly design continued filling the atmosphere with the glory and illumination of God until the entire temple was saturated with the appearance and revelation of His glory. That is the fashion of Heaven that is to be transferred to the earth— another end-time mandate is to create an atmosphere on the earth that is consistent with His nature and character in which He can dwell.

If we can fulfill these responsibilities, all other purposes and desires will be established naturally. They will be achieved by His Presence and anointing resting in us. We must likewise become the instruments that create a similar atmosphere on earth so He can tabernacle in us and accomplish all that He has foretold for this generation.

The final mandate for winning the lost and healing the sick will inherently take place because of the evidence of God's glory resting on the Lord's friends who experience close encounters with Him. We are given the incredible opportunity in this generation to function under the principles of the Kingdom of Heaven and experience intimacy with God and demonstrate the powers of the age to come.

CHAPTER 13

A NEW DAY DAWNING

THE COMING DAYS will bring greater dimensions of darkness in the world, yet our hope is for the appearing of God's weighty Presence (see Isa. 60:1-5). There is something of vital importance that we must obtain in this season that is essential to move forward.

THE OPEN DOOR

As emphasized in Revelation 3:20, the Lord stands at the door and knocks, and to him who hears and opens the Lord will come in to dine. This is an individual commission and requires an individual response. On the other side of the "open door," we will discover Living Word revelation vital for this season and God's heavenly blueprints.

> ON THE OTHER SIDE OF THE "OPEN DOOR," WE WILL DISCOVER LIVING WORD REVELATION VITAL FOR THIS SEASON AND GOD'S HEAVENLY BLUEPRINTS.

The fullness of the ministry model God has ordained to respond to the great needs and challenges of the 21st century is not presently on the Earth. It is something that we must obtain from behind the veil in the unseen realm. It is the hidden manna reserved and set apart for this generation that will equip the Bride of Christ without spot or wrinkle and empower her for the harvest.

Hebrews 8:4-5 tells us how Moses discovered the heavenly pattern for his generation.

> *Now if He were on earth, He would not be a priest at all, since there are those who offer the gifts according to the Law; who serve a copy and shadow of the heavenly things, just as Moses was warned by God when he was about to erect the tabernacle; for, "See," He says, "that you make all things according to the pattern which was shown you on the mountain."*

Moses was oftentimes required at the most inopportune times to pull aside and ascend God's mountain to receive insight, instruction, and empowerment. It was on the mountain that Moses obtained the heavenly pattern for the Tabernacle and God's ordained order of worship. So it is today.

LESSONS LEARNED

Our highest purpose is to have relationship with Him. Intimacy with the Lord is the essence of our design in creation and the highest purpose in the restoration of all things. To walk with God in the "cool of the day" is still our foremost aspiration. It is in that place of "union" that we are empowered to influence our culture and manifest His Kingdom.

The earth is entering a season of travail. World systems will be powerless in responding to the needs that are about to be present on earth. Only when anointed with the Holy Spirit can the Church impart wisdom and revelation that will provide genuine light in this dark generation!

The day is fast approaching when the prophetic ministry of the Church will once again encounter the "prophets of Baal" in a Mount Carmel showdown. God promised to send the spirit and power of Elijah before "the great and terrible day of the Lord." May it rest upon many as we contend for this higher standard!

When the genuine is present, it makes the counterfeit appear all the more perverted. The Church should not fear to take the prophetic Gospel to the marketplace where our enemy is presently attempting—often successfully— to dominate. This generation is desperate for authentic spiritual representation from the Kingdom of Light.

THE NOBILITY OF MICAIAH

In another Old Testament example, the 400 prophets of Ahab each received spiritual revelation containing measures of truth, yet the origin was a deceiving spirit the Lord allowed because of Ahab's unrighteous leadership. Micaiah, a true prophet of God, was then summoned who was able to soar above the deceiving spirit and receive a true revelation from God's heart (see 1 Kings 22:1-28).

Despite intense political pressure and the demand to conform to the wishes of illegitimate leadership, Micaiah makes this profound and revealing statement, *"As the Lord lives, what the Lord says to me, that I shall speak"* (1 Kings 22:14). May the Lord raise up many in our day like this great prophet who refused to compromise for political correctness or personal popularity.

Spiritual discernment and a good foundation in truth will clearly identify false revelation. This will motivate the radical remnant to press in all the more earnestly to receive the genuine. The Spirit of Truth will render the false spirits of revelation powerless, as with Paul, Elijah, and other loyal servants of the Lord. Instead of their prophecies bringing disillusionment and fear to many, those with the true revelatory mantles will portray courage and illumination. These will be like an immovable stake driven in the ground that will produce disarray in the enemy's camp. Light will always dispel darkness. Amen.

> THOSE WITH THE TRUE REVELATORY MANTLES WILL PORTRAY COURAGE AND ILLUMINATION.

DAVID'S EXAMPLE

Although David's destiny was one of greatness and divine favor, he was required to endure times of separation and hardship before being released into the fullness of his calling. It was during these difficult times that character was forged to prepare him for his place as king. Decisions he made in the wilderness formulated the pattern of David's life when he ascended to the throne.

A similar situation has occurred for many in the Church. It appears our enemies are prevailing, despite great promises given to us by the Holy Spirit. However, it is during times of disappointment and hardship that divine character is formed; we are purged and purified from our own carnal plans and agendas and equipped to faithfully accommodate the anointing. Righteous decisions that are made during these dry intervals will reap immeasurable dividends throughout the coming seasons of great prosperity that we are transitioning into.

While experiencing the baptism of trials, it has been challenging to wait upon the Lord for His perfect timing in releasing all His promises. Like David, we cry out to the Lord, "How long must we endure these difficult and trying times?" Patiently, the Lord admonishes us to "be still" and wait for the completion of His sanctifying work of grace within. This allows the full release of His anointing through us. That time has now arrived for the remnant.

Very often our tendency during these times has been to "do something." We often misinterpret ministry activity as "doing the will of the Father" and confuse endless motion with progress. In Matthew 7, Jesus describes many who were involved in ministry but their eternal destiny was outer darkness.

Not everyone who says to Me, "Lord, Lord," will enter the kingdom of heaven, but he who does the will of My Father who is in heaven (Matthew 7:21).

In doing the Father's will, we access the Kingdom of Heaven and find favor and grace during times of need. One of the Hebrew terms translated as *salvation* is *yeshuash,* which denotes "deliverance, welfare, prosperity, and victory." Its unique application bespeaks deliverance from present troubles and the assurance that the Lord is aware of our condition and will intervene on our behalf. He assures us:

"I know the plans that I have for you," declares the Lord, "plans for welfare and not for calamity to give you a future and a hope" (Jeremiah 29:11).

Our Savior's plans for us include welfare and prosperity, not calamity. However, wilderness experiences were allowed to establish godly character and to sow seeds of righteousness that reap bountiful dividends in the seasons ahead. We must pray with the same assurance as David, despite the external circumstances, and trustingly realize that the Lord is faithful to His promises. Not one of His promises has ever failed in all of history.

> WILDERNESS EXPERIENCES WERE
> ALLOWED TO ESTABLISH GODLY
> CHARACTER AND TO SOW SEEDS OF
> RIGHTEOUSNESS THAT REAP BOUNTIFUL
> DIVIDENDS IN THE SEASONS AHEAD.

BEHOLDING GOD'S BEAUTY

After years of walking with the Lord, David gave expression to his heart's longing. He had ultimately concluded there was only one thing he truly desired and one thing that would fully satisfy the purpose of his life—to dwell in the house of the Lord all the days of his life, to behold the Lord's beauty and meditate in His temple (see Ps. 27:4).

David's passion was to gaze upon and perceive the Lord's beauty and delight in His loveliness. His expression signifies an experiential comprehension of the beauty realm of Heaven. Can we behold the King in all His beauty?

In Isaiah 33:14-15, the Holy Spirit through the prophet Isaiah asks a revealing question: "Who can live with continual burning?" Or, in other words, who can live in an atmosphere where there are perpetual expressions of God's justice? The prophet provides the answers:

1. The one who walks righteously.

2. The one who speaks with sincerity.

3. The one who rejects unjust gain.

4. The one who shakes his hands so that they hold no bribe.

5. The one who stops his ears from hearing about bloodshed.

6. The one who shuts his eyes from looking upon evil.

Such a person lives in a state of consecration and purity, which allows them to dwell in the heavenly heights; their refuge will be the impregnable Rock. Such a person's heavenly bread will be provided and their spiritual water source will be sure. Such a person's eyes will see the King in all of His beauty and will behold the far-distant land (see Isa. 33:14-17).

Although the Lord first appeared as the suffering Lamb, He is now being revealed as the victorious King. Presently, Heaven is unveiling the Lord's great glory and kingly authority. It is our outstanding privilege to possess anointed eyes to see, behold, and perceive the revelation of the King and His Kingdom design. We are charged to be a voice on the Earth to convey our revelations from heavenly realms and give birth to this new day.

> ALTHOUGH THE LORD FIRST APPEARED AS THE SUFFERING LAMB, HE IS NOW BEING REVEALED AS THE VICTORIOUS KING.

TO BEHOLD BY REVELATION

It is vital in this day that we see by revelation. According to biblical scholars, the Hebrew word *chazah* means "to see, behold, or select for oneself." It appears fifty-four times, in every period of biblical Hebrew. *Chazah* literally signifies the ability to see "in a prophetic vision or as a seer in an ecstatic state." In Numbers 24:4, the word means to "see by way of a prophet's vision, to see with intelligence and by an experience."

> *The oracle of him who hears the words of God,*
> *who sees the vision of the Almighty, falling*
> *down, yet having his eyes uncovered.*

Through weighty biblical promises, we are given opportunities to experientially apprehend God's glory attributes in perceptible and tangible ways. We do this by learning the art of "waiting" upon Him to behold His beauty and meditate on Him. The sum of David's passions was captured in that one thing.

May it also be the chief desire of the Lord's Bride to see, behold, comprehend, and explore the mysteries and infinite riches of the Lord's goodness and beauty! There we discover His plans and purposes for this unique hour in which we live! Then we can build according to God's ordained model and facilitate the Lord's last-day plans.

CHAPTER 14

MANTLES OF REVELATION AND POWER

I HAVE FOUND the life of Joan of Arc fascinating, especially after reading Mark Twain's incredible book on her life. The Lord has been bringing this testimony to memory often in recent days, and I felt its truth is pertinent to this present transition season. We are entering a time when the deposit of God's Spirit that rested upon prior great champions will be reinstituted on those who have been prepared for them. This will be a firstfruits harvest that will provoke the body forward into a season of great harvest.

There are very valuable Kingdom principles that we can learn from the life of this wonderful prophetess. Her courage, valor, and obedience will typify many in this last-days' generation who will give themselves totally to God's plan and purpose.

THE MAID OF ORLEANS

Few women in history are as intriguing as *Jeanne D'Arc*, the French peasant girl born in 1412, who heard and obeyed Heaven. To some she was a saint, to others a heretic, but history chronicles her as emerging from obscurity to become her nation's youngest military leader.

In 15 months she changed the course of European history. Her eventual martyrdom was satan's attempt to destroy her divine gift. Even so, many of today's champions can inherit similar mantles of leadership and power through the Lord's principles of justice. God said, "I will restore!"

A SUPERNATURAL VOICE

For her, the unlikely destiny began one summer afternoon at the age of 13.

On that fateful day she saw a brilliant light and heard the audible voice of the Archangel Michael, leader of God's armies. Michael addressed her as "Joan the Maid" with the added admonition to live a pure and virtuous life. He announced her destiny as a God-appointed deliverer to lead the army of France. Joan reported, "I recognized that it was the voice of an angel. This voice has always guarded me well and I have always understood it; it instructed me to be good and to go to church often."

To Joan, the voices of God's spiritual messengers could be distinguished in the same fashion as one person communicates with another. She received audible instructions from the spiritual realm that charged her with the formidable task of uniting a fragmented army and ultimately altering the fate and leadership of her nation.

A DELIVERER IS BORN

The extreme hardship of one hundred years of war with England preceded the appearance of Joan. The English occupied considerable portions of France with plans of further expansion until the prophetess shifted the momentum to the French.

The messengers of Heaven conveyed to her a twofold commission: first, to lead an army against the English in defense of Orleans, a crucial and strategic city for the French; and second, to restore the throne to its rightful heir, the Dauphin of France, a term used to identify the heir apparent who later became Charles VII.

France had not had a crowned king since the death of Charles VI in 1422. Instead, the French crown had passed to the infant King Henry VI of England through a treaty signed by Charles VI.

This twofold mandate was an unthinkable task for an illiterate teenager living in the 15th century. Even so, the messengers from Heaven gave explicit directions. Joan possessed the uncanny willingness to risk life and limb in obedience to their instructions. She relinquished herself totally to the cause of Heaven that launched her into this supernatural arena.

THE MANDATE ESTABLISHED

To share this vision with the Dauphin of France, Joan journeyed over 300 miles through enemy territory for her first encounter with Charles VII. Charles actually staged a test to determine the authenticity of her revelations.

When Joan entered the huge meeting hall filled with over 300 guests, the Dauphin was not seated on his throne. Instead, he was dressed as a commoner and had mingled with the crowd. Led by her supernatural council, Joan walked directly to Charles and addressed him as the imminent leader of France. Moreover, she also divulged divine insight involving his life known only to him and God. This validated for the eventual king that Joan of Arc was no ordinary maiden.

Subsequently, Charles and his councilmen embraced her vision and allowed her to lead 4,000 troops in support of the besieged city of Orleans on April 29, 1429. The victory was swift and sure!

Phenomenal Victories

After capturing smaller forts that bordered Orleans, Joan surrounded the occupied city and led the assault against the English. Joan was gravely wounded in the conflict, as she had earlier predicted. Nevertheless, by the end of the day she returned to the battle. The mere sight of their courageous leader rallied the French army who promptly routed the remaining English forces. So moved were these hardened soldiers by Joan's anointing and heroism that they "gave up swearing and prostitutes and committed themselves to a virtuous life."

Joan insisted the men under her charge conduct themselves in a manner becoming professional soldiers.

She allowed no swearing or lewd behavior and expected commendable character. The men willingly followed her leadership and affectionately bestowed on her the title "maid of Orleans."

In subsequent weeks, Joan and her army liberated several other French cities enduring English occupation. So convincing were the early victories that in one confrontation only three French soldiers perished compared to over 2,000 English casualties.

After accepting the surrender of Troyes, Joan persuaded Charles to return to Rheims for his royal coronation. In fulfillment of Joan's directive given by the Lord through heavenly messengers, Charles VII was officially recognized as monarch of France.

HER BETRAYAL AND DEATH

Despite her conquests, betrayal from French leaders led to Joan's capture—this too according to her own predictions. In embarrassment, English rulers determined to prove her success resulted from witchcraft and sorcery. They added to her charges heresy—the act of challenging the authority of the church. The representatives of the church who tried her believed God spoke only to priests. It flew in the face of their belief system for God to communicate directly with individuals.

For nearly five months, Joan of Arc was imprisoned, not in a facility for women but with English soldiers. Nevertheless, strengthened by the Lord and His heavenly messengers, she remained steadfast throughout the ordeal.

To validate the charge of heresy, the English employed clergyman and theologians who strenuously examined Joan with the malicious intent of discrediting her testimony. Remarkably, her wise and skillful answers alleviated their entrapping questions. According to Joan, heavenly messengers regularly brought to her God's perfect council.

Ultimately, the tainted court rendered a guilty verdict and condemned Joan to be burned at the stake. At 9 A.M. on May 30, 1431, the 19-year-old messenger of God was wrongfully executed. As the flames began to consume her body, a cross held before her eyes was Joan's sole request. Her final word was the name Jesus.

Five hundred years after being burned at the stake for heresy, Joan of Arc is declared a saint and is revered by the country she saved.

A CALL FOR JUSTICE

The loving eyes of our heavenly Judge see and record every action of humanity. In this end-time generation, the books of Heaven will be opened and restitution offered for injustices committed against God's covenant people.

As with Joan of Arc, satan has battled the saints of God for millennia and seemingly prevailed. Nevertheless, God, as the Righteous Judge, will render a final verdict on behalf of the saints. Daniel recorded:

> *I kept looking, and that horn was waging war*
> *with the saints and overpowering them until*
> *the Ancient of Days came and judgment was*

passed in favor of the saints of the Highest One, and the time arrived when the saints took possession of the kingdom (Daniel 7:21-22).

Divine justice, released in this age, will be a key to empower God's people. Joan of Arc's life was a prophetic model. There will be many who follow her standard with faithful and obedient hearts and commissioned in awesome ways. Every seemingly lost commission, anointing, and spiritual gift will be redeemed and released to willing recipients.

> DIVINE JUSTICE, RELEASED IN THIS AGE, WILL BE A KEY TO EMPOWER GOD'S PEOPLE.

For thousands of years, God's children have been martyred, persecuted, and plundered, but heavenly justice will decree that all be fully restored and compensated.

All things take place under the all-seeing eye of God, and He has promised to restore all that our adversary has ruined. Clearly Joan and others like her received a martyr's reward in eternity. Moreover, they sowed spiritual seeds that will reap the most outstanding deposit of divine grace never before demonstrated.

I WILL RESTORE

The Joel 2:25 promise of restoration is one of the paramount passages of this day. God pledges:

I will restore to you the years that the swarming locust has eaten, the crawling locust, the

consuming locust, and the chewing locust, My
great army which I sent among you (Joel 2:25
NKJV).

Joan of Arc was God's appointed representative during
a crucial juncture in human history. Abuse of authority
from corrupt political officials eradicated the heavenly
deposit entrusted to her. God's just nature will mandate
a manifold restoration of this and other lost anointing
through faithful and obedient vessels prepared to
apprehend and demonstrate this destiny and the Lord's
redemptive virtues. The Lord will render a verdict in favor
of His people as the Supreme Judge of all creation.

THE SEVENFOLD
REVELATION OF HIS GLORY

Apocalypse is a Greek term meaning "the unveiling,
disclosure, and making known of something previously
veiled." That is the term used in the title of the last book of
the Bible—the Unveiling/Revelation of Jesus Christ.

Almost daily I am reading and/or listening to this
fascinating and glorious book of the Bible. One thing is
certain that I have discovered over the course of these
days—we are imminently facing a tremendous and
unprecedented revelation, unveiling, and disclosure of
the Lord Jesus Christ to our generation. Like John, our
understanding of who the Lord is and the power He
embodies will now be taken to an all new level.

Clearly, John, "the disciple whom Jesus loved," had a
great measure of understanding involving the Lord and

His Person. After all, he had walked with Him for three years on the earth and witnessed the crucifixion and His glorious resurrection. Following the Day of Pentecost, John became one with God's Spirit and walked with Him for six decades before finding himself exiled to Patmos.

It was on Patmos that John had this fantastic visitation that no doubt forever changed his perspective and understanding of who Jesus really is. Even all the years of walking with the Lord and witnessing His Spirit's work did not prepare John for what he witnessed in that encounter. He saw the Lord as the Overcoming King and Righteous Judge, and the power of it struck John to the ground as a dead man. It was as though the Lord had to reveal Himself more completely to John before he could adequately pen the words that are now in the Apocalypse. John saw:

> *Seven golden lampstands; and in the middle of the lampstands I saw one like a son of man, clothed in a robe reaching to the feet, and girded across His chest with a golden sash. His head and His hair were white like white wool, like snow; and His eyes were like a flame of fire. His feet were like burnished bronze, when it has been made to glow in a furnace, and His voice was like the sound of many waters. In His right hand He held seven stars, and out of His mouth came a sharp two-edged sword; and His face was like the sun shining in its strength.*

When I saw Him, I fell at His feet like a dead man (Revelation 1:12-17).

I believe something similar is in store for us. We cannot adequately face the challenges and mandates placed upon us for the days ahead without a more complete and thorough revelation of the Lord Jesus. Like John, the Bride of Christ desperately needs to witness the sevenfold revelation of His glory.

> THE BRIDE OF CHRIST DESPERATELY NEEDS TO WITNESS THE SEVENFOLD REVELATION OF HIS GLORY.

REVELATION OF JESUS THE JUST JUDGE

Both Daniel and John were given phenomenal revelatory encounters with the Lord in His attributes as the Just Judge. His judgments are perfect and His ways are beyond the scrutiny of man. His mysteries embody a promise for the welfare of His people and the unfolding of His Kingdom on earth. The mystery of His justice will unlock the virtue of Heaven for this purpose.

The supernatural visitation awarded to the apostle John while on Patmos distinguishes in great narrative form the different aspects of His qualities in justice. John saw the Lord adorned in His royal attire representing the constitution of His authority and kingly reign.

His Hair as a White Snow

The symbolic depiction of this image involving the Lord's hair communicates the supreme wisdom by which He judges the affairs of mankind. The people of Israel vividly remembered the glory once resident in their nation through the leadership of Solomon. The heavenly impartation of wisdom given to this king became legendary. Nonetheless, a greater King than Solomon has now come. The One who is the very source of all wisdom will judge from the books of Heaven involving the issues of mankind and the restoration of lost heritage.

Both John and Daniel saw the purity of God's wisdom in His justice portrayed through hair as white as snow. He revealed Himself as the suffering Lamb; now we will see demonstrations of the overcoming King who comes to wage war with His enemies and render justice (see Rev. 19:11).

> WE WILL SEE DEMONSTRATIONS OF THE OVERCOMING KING WHO COMES TO WAGE WAR WITH HIS ENEMIES AND RENDER JUSTICE.

His Eyes as Flames of Fire

The penetrating and fiery eyes of Jesus the Just Judge have seen all that has taken place in the realm of mankind. Nothing has escaped His notice, nor have the motives and thoughts resident in the hearts of people. Our thoughts are louder in Heaven than our words on the earth.

The eyes of God have roved to and fro throughout the earth to record every act of righteousness and document every injustice committed against the heritage of Christ. Not one will go without restitution and restoration. The sevenfold Spirit of God embodies the all-seeing eyes of God.

> *For who has despised the day of small things? But these seven will be glad when they see the plumb line in the hand of Zerubbabel—these are the eyes of the Lord which range to and fro throughout the earth* (Zechariah 4:10).

Feet of Burnished Bronze

His feet of burnished bronze represent His right to stand in judgment. Bronze is a very hard substance that has been tried by fire. The sinless, spotless Son of God endured the harshness and recompense of iniquity and transgression on behalf of lost mankind. The fiery furnace of God's wrath against sin was heaped upon the Lord Jesus. He took it to the cross and won the right to release justice in the earth.

> *Because He has fixed a day in which He will judge the world in righteousness through a Man whom He has appointed, having furnished proof to all men by raising Him from the dead* (Acts 17:31).

His feet will stand upon the land and sea to surrender justice in the realm of man. Only He can carry the burden of authority for this royal responsibility because of the great price that was paid for our redemption. The prophet

Moses prophetically saw the Lord coming in His glory, revealing the attributes of both mercy and justice. As the Lord passed before Moses He declared His eternal qualities of compassion and grace. He is slow to anger and abounding in lovingkindness and truth. He extends mercy and forgiveness to thousands, pardoning iniquity, transgression, and sin, but he will by no means leave the guilt of sin unpunished.

If sin and transgression has been released to the Lord Jesus through His blood then there remains no judgment for sin. Justice then relinquishes blessings, favor, and grace to the righteous.

Voice as the Sound of Many Waters

Waters very often symbolically point to the multitudes of peoples and nations. Likewise, His voice is the voice of ultimate authority and power. Throughout the ages a prophetic message has been delegated and entrusted to each generation through God's messengers. There has been an allotted portion of heavenly manna deposited throughout each juncture of church history.

The prophet Daniel in his prayer of repentance recognized that his generation did not obey the voice of the Lord presented to them through His servants the prophets. He acknowledged:

> Nor have we obeyed the voice of the Lord our God, to walk in His teachings which He set before us through His servants the prophets (Daniel 9:10).

When the day of justice arrives, every voice that has declared the revelation of God to their generation will be sounded as one. That voice will be the voice of the Holy Spirit rendering justice.

In His Right Hand, Seven Stars

The Holy Spirit has utilized the agency of man to articulate His voice. The seven stars are the ambassadors of Heaven who carried and imparted the revelation of Jesus to their generation. The Scriptures plainly emphasize the meaning of the seven stars as messengers.

Clearly, the apostle Paul was a messenger and voice to the early church who worked in cooperation with the Holy Spirit and the hosts of Heaven. The message was oftentimes communicated to him and the apostle John through spiritual beings who embodied God's revelations. That pattern continued throughout the Church ages and will be emphasized in this day. An accentuation of this reality has been plainly recorded in history. Martin Luther was a messenger to his day, heralding the truth that the just shall live by faith. The progressive recovery of lost heritage continued through the messengers of the next generation including John Wesley, George Whitefield, John Knox, and many others.

Likewise, the development of the 20th century also produced key prophetic voices who were pioneers who burned with a message of truth that could not be contained. The ministry of healing was restored to the corporate body along with the baptism of the Holy

Spirit witnessed at the Azuza Street mission. Finally, this generation will experience a company of messengers who not only impart a truth but embody the Truth. That is our promise and legacy.

> THIS GENERATION WILL EXPERIENCE A COMPANY OF MESSENGERS WHO NOT ONLY IMPART A TRUTH BUT EMBODY THE TRUTH. THAT IS OUR PROMISE AND LEGACY.

Two-edged Sword

The living Word is quick and powerful and sharper than a two-edged sword. Only the Lord can separate spirit from soul. He is the one who discerns the thoughts and intentions of our hearts. The Lord Jesus has the unique ability to examine and weigh our motives to determine if we are capable of carrying the authority of Heaven to our generation.

It is His intent and desire to live in and among His people bringing the revelation of Himself and His Word. The Book of Revelation depicts the Lord Jesus coming on a white horse with the declaration that He is faithful and true. Embroidered on His garment is the depiction of His person—the Word of God. The Word became flesh and dwelt among mankind. He once again desires to do the same through His body.

Face Like the Sun

Resident in the Lord are His manifold holy attributes. Many people still envision the Lord as a baby in a manger. However, He is now an awesome, victorious, overcoming King—great is His power and authority to be administered and experientially apprehended on the earth in a demonstration of His victory.

The Son of Righteousness will arise with healing in His wings to bring a fresh revelation of His Person to the earth. The residue of glory resting on Moses after his face-to-face encounters with God overwhelmed the people of Israel. He was forced to cover his face because of the tangible impartation of heavenly virtue that he conveyed. How much more in this generation when the Lord demonstrates His victory and imparts His glory within His Bride! Then the voice of the Bride will be heard in a profound display of glory. Christ in us—the hope of glory. This endowment will come to those who view Him with an unveiled face.

ABOUT PAUL KEITH DAVIS

PAUL KEITH DAVIS has written five books and numerous articles appearing in various Christian publications, including the *MorningStar Journal*, *Charisma*, and *Church Growth International*. Paul Keith travels extensively, speaking at conferences and churches, imparting the end-time mandate of preparation for the glory and manifest presence of Christ. His heart's desire is to see the full restoration of biblical apostolic ministry manifested through the Spirit of Truth residing in God's people, expressing salvation, healing, and deliverance to the glory of God and His Christ. He and his wife Amy oversee WhiteDove Ministries based out of Orange Beach, Alabama.